JOHN —

ALWAYS BE A

GREAT DUCK !

Denton

IT NEVER RAINS IN AUTZEN STADIUM

THE DON ESSIG STORY

By Chuck Wenstrom

Book design by Tom Penix
tompenix@gmail.com
www.penwaxdesign.com

Cover photo by Chris Pietsch
chris@ChrisPietschMedia.com
www.ChrisPietschMedia.com

Back cover photo by Sally Klein

All inside photos courtesy of The Essig family

McArthur Court photo (p. 121) courtesy of *The Register-Guard*

The Lone Deranger photo (p. 121) courtesy of Ken Hoiland

ISBN: 978-0-9883329-1-1
Printed in Eugene, Oregon
by QSL Print Communications

Thank you to the University of Oregon and the Marketing
& Brand Management department for permission to use all
UO trademarks found in this book.

For ordering information, contact:
itneverrains45@gmail.com

Dedication

*This book is dedicated to our closest and best friends:
Janet Essig and Joanne Wenstrom.*

Table of Contents

	Preface	13
CHAPTER ONE	The Chicago Connection	19
CHAPTER TWO	Going to Oregon State	27
CHAPTER THREE	Back to Oregon City	41
CHAPTER FOUR	On to Eugene	51
CHAPTER FIVE	Public Address Announcing	59
CHAPTER SIX	Organization Development Program	67
CHAPTER SEVEN	Howard Elementary School	73
CHAPTER EIGHT	North Eugene High School	85
CHAPTER NINE	Moving to District Office	101
CHAPTER TEN	On the Road to a Consulting Business	107
CHAPTER ELEVEN	A Career in Consulting	113
CHAPTER TWELVE	Scenes from McArthur Court	121
CHAPTER THIRTEEN	"The Man in the Sky"	129
CHAPTER FOURTEEN	Don Essig Announcing Statistics	141
	Post Script from the Author	143

Acknowledgements

I have to acknowledge the time and effort Don Essig spent in recalling for me his life's endeavors and accomplishments in my preparing and writing this biography. I may have been overzealous in prodding and urging him to send me more information about his life's journey as a young boy, a student, a teacher and administrator, an organizer, an accomplished public speaker, and "The Voice of the Ducks."

It's also important to recognize his contributions to the University of Oregon as well as to the Eugene School District in other ways than with the UO Athletic Department where he spent some 45-plus years as a public address announcer for athletic events I have to say, "Thanks, Don, for sharing your life story."

I have to again thank my wife, Joanne, for putting up with me for yet another book and for her editorial assistance. She worked as a secretary in an Oregon State University news information office and it shows!

Thanks, Sally Klein, for ongoing encouragement and assistance with the creation of this book.

Kudos to Gina Hoppe in the OSU Alumni Center, and to Stuart Burke at Beaver Sports Properties in the OSU Athletic Department, who did some invaluable research providing information for me to use in this biography.

There have to be accolades to "Aunt Janny," Don's better-half, for just always being there to help, and making sure no rain would fall on this manuscript.

Foreward

Putting aside the rain in Autzen Stadium, this is about my life growing up as well as maturing on a small farm outside Oregon City, Oregon. It includes undergraduate days at Oregon State College, 30 years of experiences in the education profession as an elementary teacher, elementary and high school principal, and school district administrator. Also included is information about my years as a Master and PhD student at the University of Oregon. In the mix was 25 years as a human relations consultant in the USA, Canada and Europe.

There are many references in the book to a number of positive relationships I have formed over the years with many friends athletic directors, and coaches, as well as a large number of fans. After accepting the public address announcing position in 1967, I made a commitment to the University of Oregon to be a strong supporter of their many programs, both academic and athletic. Those activities included many years of fundraising, serving as the President of the Eugene/Springfield Oregon Club, being a member of the UO Alumni Board of Directors, and serving on the College of Education Dean's Advisory Council.

My life goal of helping others improve their personal and professional lives becomes evident through my writing, my teaching, and my consulting work. This is a basic life theme that evolved from my childhood experiences though my parents, grandparents, teachers and an abundance of close friends, as well as through my own family relationships.

Interspersed throughout the book's chapters are citations about my philosophies and how I was able to apply my own learning in life and extend that to my many friends, colleagues, clients and fans.

I am very thankful to have close friends Sherryl Barnum, Bob Morris and Jeanne Brewer, who were willing to edit the manuscript. All of them added to the content as well as making other needed changes. A special thanks to Tom Penix for the creative development of the cover and paging of the book. His knowledge and talent in book creation definitely contributed to its overall professional appearance.

Best friends Don & Chuck

My close friend, Chuck Wenstrom deserves much gratitude for encouraging me to let him write this book. He has done the creative job of relating my wide variety of life experiences through his extensive vocabulary and sense of humor. He has made this book a fun read to learn more about the "Man behind the voice in Autzen Stadium, McArthur Court, and Matthew Knight Arena."

Don Essig

Preface

You might think that Don Essig is all wet when he expounds "It never rains in Autzen Stadium!" Well, he's not if you follow along with Bob Welch, columnist for Oregon's *Eugene Register-Guard* newspaper. Bob writes that it's been a 8.7% chance of rain in the University of Oregon's Autzen Stadium since 1990, and a 35.9% incidence of sun-filled days in the stadium, also during this time. Incidentally, 1990 is the year Essig made his prognostication concerning rain from his press-box perch in reaction to a new stadium policy that banned the use of umbrellas during game days.

So how did this self-proclaimed forecaster become such a rainy-day prophet? Mostly it was because he believed and wanted to convey to all those in attendance that rain could never dampen the spirit or the enthusiasm of Duck football fans when cheering on the home team. That is Don's forte: "Always be positive." "Have a positive day!"

All that might be true, but just the same it's easy for him to put out that no rain gibberish from his comfortable, uncrowded, warm and snug press box seat atop Autzen Stadium on the U of O campus. What about the paying folks down below in the rows of stadium seats potentially waiting out a forecasted rainy-day Saturday? True Duck fans obviously understand the point he is trying to put across.

With that in mind, go about 50 miles northwest to the sleepy town of Corvallis, where Oregon State University Beaver football fans were to go through the same rainy day transformation. Give or take a few years. In 1998, after 20 years of consistent losing, the Beavers came out with a 3-8 win, 5-loss home record including a double-overtime upset win over the favored Webfoots. This was followed by a 55-18 home record covering the next 10 years! So one could say, in a manner of speaking, that former Oregon Stater Essig's peremptory attitude somehow sort of rubbed off onto the Beavs, too.

Enough about this rainy-day business that occurred far into the life of Don Essig. It is time to ask a simple question, "How can a person write a book about a best friend, now a Duck but also a former Beaver, who is a renowned public figure in University of Oregon athletics, a preeminent Oregon educator, and a presenter of management and organization development courses worldwide since 1971?" You can throw in public address announcing, with a figurative title, "Voice of the Ducks," that Don has been doing at the University of Oregon since 1967, longer than any other PA announcer in the PAC-12!

This makes it tough to point out that at least 3 times a year, when the Ducks and Beavers meet in football and basketball rivalries, and to a lesser extent in other athletic confrontations, Don becomes a traitor, a villain and an all-around bad guy, to some Oregon Staters.

It has to be remembered there was a time when Don Essig acted out at Oregon State College as an undergraduate; popular student, ambitious, Rally Squad leader, and an all-around good guy! What happened? He attended graduate school at the University of Oregon, obtained a Doctorate in Organization Development, and became recognized by all Duck fans as the "Voice of the Ducks" through his public address announcing. That's what happened!

In between, and among all the hoopla, Don was an elementary school teacher and principal, as well as being a high school principal; ran his own consulting business even while heading up management development programs for Eugene public schools. He also became a nationally recognized motivational speaker.

Some fellow Beavers who are caught up in and follow along with those folks unhappy with Don Essig's Beaver-to-Duck transformation are just going to have to adjust, get on with their own lives, and accept the fact that Webfoot people really aren't all that bad. Many of them, too, are former Beavers!

In 2010 Don returned to his Oregon State alma mater for initiation into the Golden Jubilee Association for his 1960 graduating class. He was asked to MC the 50-year reunion dinner with, according to Don's faulty recollection, the stipulation he not wear any green and yellow.

Wrong! It would easily have been accepted, according to his own often stated belief, "Making Life an Opportunity, Not a Burden." This would just reiterate how far and how diversified members of his class of 1960 had travelled and what they accomplished to attain their goals. Even as far away as Eugene, and as some hard-assed Beaver believers would suggest, the home of "that evil empire"—University of Oregon.

Don has to be reminded that Thomas John Autzen graduated from Oregon Agricultural College (now OSU) with a BS in Mechanical/Electrical Engineering in 1909. He became wealthy with his many business successes, and in the 1950s he established the Autzen Foundation. His son, Thomas Edward Autzen, became president.

In the 1960s the philanthropic Autzen Foundation donated $250,000 to build a new football stadium at the University of Oregon. T.J. died in 1958, so his son T.E. was most instrumental in contributing "by far the largest donation to the project!" The stadium was most properly named "Thomas J. Autzen Stadium."

There is a short postscript here. Thomas Edward Autzen is a 1943 graduate of University of Oregon. He died in 1997. However, just for the record, in the late 1990s the playing field at Autzen was officially named "Rich Brooks' Field" after a popular Oregon State Beaver football player who later became the head football coach for the Oregon Ducks, a post he had held for 18 years.

Another example of switching state loyalties: Mike Parker, a popular and legendary "Voice of the Beavers" for the Beaver Nation, graduated from University of Oregon. By the same token, Mike Stone, current public address announcer for the Beavs, is a

UO graduate. Go back to Ron Finley, a standout wrestler for Dale Thomas at Oregon State, who took over the Duck grappler program, which he headed up for 25 years! And, so it goes.

The orange-black to yellow-green and vice versa has a long tradition.

It harkens back to Don's own words: when opportunity presents itself, go for it, even if the obstacles seem real, or are imagined prejudices.

Don was asked at the reunion how many more years he would be public address announcing at Autzen Stadium, McArthur Court, or eventually, Matthew Knight Arena.

"Actually, this is my forty-eighth year counting from 1962 when I started announcing at Oregon City High School. Anyway, it would be nice finishing up 50 years for the Ducks; then I will start thinking about retiring and giving up my choice Press Box seats in Matthew Knight Arena, as well as in Autzen Stadium."

Right: Don at
age 5, in Dallas

Below: Article
sent to Don from
his father

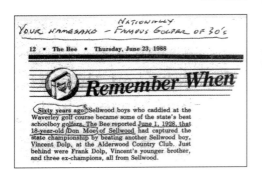

NATIONALLY
YOUR NAMESAKE — FAMOUS GOLFER OF 30's

12 • The Bee • Thursday, June 23, 1988

Remember When

Sixty years ago: Sellwood boys who caddied at the
Waverley golf course became some of the state's best
schoolboy golfers. The Bee reported June 1, 1928, that
18-year-old Don Moe of Sellwood had captured the
state championship by beating another Sellwood boy,
Vincent Dolp, at the Alderwood Country Club. Just
behind were Frank Dolp, Vincent's younger brother,
and three ex-champions, all from Sellwood.

Above:
Don's 8th-grade
graduation,
seated front row
left

Right: Don's
"non-retired" #54
jersey

CHAPTER ONE

The Chicago Connection

"My parents gave me the greatest gift anyone could give another person — they believed in me."

—Jim Valvano
College basketball coach

As in all biographies it has to come down to a beginning. For Don, the Essig story had its start in England in 1781 with the birth of George Essex, Don's Great-Great-Great Grandfather. His work in later life was for the King's "Geographics," making maps for British possessions throughout the world. In Germany, George met a young lass who said she would not marry him unless he changed his name from Essex to Essig. He made the change and the rest is history for Don and his clan.

All the Essigs from this early beginning were blessed and given baptism in the "Congregational and Christian Churches," according to William F. Essig, Don's Grandfather, who had written of his own Grandfather.

Grandpa William came to America from Germany in 1884 with his father, mother and family. He eventually became an ordained minister, serving in numerous churches throughout the United

States. His "Ninth Charge" was to Park Ridge, Illinois' Immanuel Congregational Church. It was here in Chicago that the Essig saga, now known and accepted by the family, had its beginning. Although it might be difficult to believe, the family still thinks that Chicago's world-famous O'Hare Airport should have the name "Essig" posted on it somewhere.

Why?

Don tells the story. His father, Milton Essig, was born in Park Ridge, Illinois, smack-dab in the middle of what was to become Chicago's "Orchard Field," an airplane landing area. The City of Chicago razed the house where Dad Essig was brought into this world and on it was built the "Orchard" airfield. Later, this site was made into a major international airport.

The Essig family has chosen to remember and be loyal to the old family homestead, and aren't taking the naming of this now famous plot of land sitting down. In their hearts and minds the Essig name should be attached somewhere to the airport: "Essig International," or "Essig Field," or "Essig Runway," or Essig something. Word is the family wants to take this naming matter up with the Chicago Mayor and City Council to have a name insertion somewhere, when feasible. Don says he is going to stick by his family's guns concerning this very valuable piece of Essig family lore.

Chicago's major International airport was named to honor Edward "Butch" O'Hare, a World War II flying ace and a Medal of Honor recipient who was from Chicago.

Be that as it may, Grandparents Reverend Doctor William and Louise Essig were only involved in the German Zion Congregational Church in Park Ridge, and didn't know much about airports even though it seemed they never stayed very long in any one place. William was a minister and went where the people needed him to preach the word of God. Milton moved around extensively with his parents and his older brother, William, Jr. and sister, Agnes. He graduated from high school in Sheboygan, Wisconsin, while only 15 years of age, two years ahead of schedule because of his smarts.

Eventually, Grandfather Essig was called to Oregon and settled his family in Beavercreek. From here the Reverend Essig spread the Gospel throughout northwestern Oregon, on horseback. He was a preacher-man.

It was in Beavercreek that Milton met Natalie Bittner and it was in the Beavercreek Congregational Church where they were married.

Milton still had that family travel bug in him and took his family with him on various job assignments throughout western Oregon. Don was born in 1938 in Dallas and Marcus became Don's brother there in 1942.

Sister Natalie came along in Portland in 1946.

It was about this time that Mother Natalie and Milton decided to buy a farm at Beavercreek near Oregon City. Don had attended grade school in Portland before going to Beavercreek School, where he was enrolled in third grade. Earlier he had attended first grade at the old Francis Willard School in Eugene, which later burned down. It is ironic and one might suppose fitting that Don later taught at the new Francis Willard School from 1966 to 1969.

The family had now come together on the farm. Dad Essig had by this time seen some promise in son Don's voice. He was strongly urged, as he confided later, to have some cows, chickens and some rabbits for Don to care for and manage on the farm as he was the oldest. This way, according to Milton, Don could also use his pervasive and persuasive voice to at first call the cows. Milton started with the cows, adding to the farm the chickens and rabbits. Then came berries and filberts along with the muscle chore for Don of hauling hay for the cows. To add to the voice issue, Dad signed Don up to sing in the church choir, that Milton directed.

The Essig family was very much church-oriented. Grandfather William was the pastor of the Church in Beavercreek. From choir practice Thursday nights, there was Sunday morning class followed by religious meetings in the church. This and the regular social gatherings, such as potlucks, made the Congregational Church the center of life for the Essigs.

Don has been a devout Protestant as a continuing member of

the Congregational Church all his life. He wrote a piece for the "My Faith" column that appeared in *The Eugene Register Guard* newspaper back in 1975. "A major part of becoming the whole Christian is learning how to reach out to and care for others, not expecting a reward, but simply doing it because it is right."

Don had six years of church camp at Camp Adams in Colton, Oregon, during late grade school and into high school. He served elected offices in the church youth program, including being a delegate to Pilgrim Fellowship Conferences in Nebraska in 1956 and in New York City in 1958.

After high school Don ended his involvement in the Pilgrim Fellowship program, but not before he created some lifetime friendships. One such friend was Chuck Hale in Eugene. Chuck took Don to the State of Oregon High School Basketball Tournament in old MacArthur Court on the University of Oregon campus. That must have hooked him because he eventually would be doing the public address for Duck home basketball games there for 43 years!

Next in the busy, early life of Don Moe Essig was taking lessons playing the piano, which he loved although it brought him inside when he rather would have been outside playing cowboys and Indians with the other kids. He tells of sitting at the piano all by himself because his teacher had such a large derriere there wasn't room for both of them on the piano stool at the same time. The solution was to get another bench, one for him and one for her. He said sometimes when he was practicing he would try to peer around her huge body to see the kids outside chasing around and playing games. He had to stay with this piano chore which was, in essence, the beginning for him of a lifetime interest and career in music.

From sophomore through his senior year at Oregon City High School, Don played the piano for church on Sunday mornings. He also continued singing in the church choir as well as in the school choir throughout his high school years. The singing and playing piano made it easy for Don to participate in Oregon City High School musicals, plays and other school stage activities.

Little did he know at the time that beginning in the mid-1980's he would be playing the University of Oregon fight song for the Eugene-Springfield Oregon Club members to sing at their weekly meetings. This has been an ongoing activity for Don to the present day.

Vestiges of Don's athletic prowess came to the fore when he was part of the Pioneer freshmen and junior varsity basketball teams. He was asked if he remembered the story of how long time Oregon State coach, Amory "Slats" Gill, would sometimes put his reserve players into storage? Did this ever happen to him?

This anecdote relates that before Oregon State's basketball coliseum (later to be known as Gill Coliseum) was built, the Beavers played in the Men's Gym at the center of campus. Next to the gymnasium floor were small rooms used for handball and racquetball. Sometimes during the game, Slats would send a little used reserve player to one of the rooms to warm up before entering the game. One time he sent a player into the racquetball room to get ready to play.

The sub dutifully went into the room and started doing jumping jacks, pushups, stretches; everything he could think of to get ready to play. He kept at this until he no longer heard any activity in the gymnasium. He peeked out the door and the teams had already left the floor and the spectators were leaving. He sheepishly beat a hasty retreat to the locker room. Slats had forgotten all about him stashed away in the racquetball room! The one-time player tells the story on himself.

Nope, Don insists this never happened to him; mostly because there weren't any side rooms directly accessible to the gym floor at Oregon City High School. However, he did let it be known that most of his game action took place at the end of the bench! He also revealed that both freshmen coach, Joe Davis, and JV coach Tom Nutter would sometimes look down the bench and wonder, "If I put Essig in the game now, can we still win?"

Don said he still felt positive and content about being on the team. Before high school most of his hoop experience was shooting baskets inside the barn loft at home after milking the cows in the evenings. Beavercreek Grade School didn't have any athletic programs, other than, maybe, softball.

During his high school junior year he tried out for varsity basketball. It didn't work out, so he quit the team. Instead he was positive he could make an impact performing in the junior class play.

He did! Could anyone believe that the play would be entitled "No More Homework," and that he was cast as the high school principal? Don's total career after graduate schools was in education: teacher, principal, university professor, and presenter (teacher) of professional management programs. Indeed, his part in that junior class play had more of an impact on him than even he himself realized at the time.

Another ambitious undertaking was to play football his senior year for the Oregon City Pioneers, but he said he didn't get to play very much. He confided that the truth of the matter was that they used him so little in practices he got most of his football exercise and workout walking home from school following practice! He lived out on the farm and they didn't have convenient school bus arrangements; it was a long walk.

When looking at the Oregon City football team photograph, Don stood out in the back proudly wearing his very prominent jersey, number 54. He said he didn't get to play in very many games, but he remained positive while waiting his turn to enter the fray from way down at the end of the bench. He admitted they never retired his Old 54, but he is quite sure they retired his spot on the bench to the woodshed because it was, literally, worn away by himself and other wannabe players waiting to be called into the game.

On the social side, dating for him in high school turned out to be almost a zero: 3 dates, 3 different girls; one time each. It's enough to make one wonder if it had anything to do with his family name change from "Essex" to Essig! Once he did get a positive on the dating scene, taking a girl to the Junior-Senior Prom! After much prompting he finally admitted that he was almost a regular lothario; well, not quite but close, at summer church camp. From here he said he gained much experience at dating, at least for one week of the year!

Working on the family farm with his Dad, part-time at the Smuckers' cannery and volunteering as president in many church and school activities helped to build a lifetime philosophy of leadership. He believed in taking care of the folks who worked with you. Having a "positive attitude" later went on to symbolize Don's life work.

Come winter of 1955 Don decided to enroll at Oregon State College. His stated purpose was to join his cousin, Bob Essig, who was already at OSC, also because many of his high school friends were planning to go to Corvallis. He had in mind becoming an architect. At a cow college? He said Oregon wouldn't have him because he lacked a foreign language requirement. Did this also hold true for public address announcers as well?

Just asking.

Some may ask from either side of the barnyard fence, how in the world did this polished, debonaire, active and well-brought-up country boy become a Beaver? For that matter, how did he ever become a Duck? Stay tuned for the best is yet to come.

Right: Don's 50-year OSC medallion and 1959 OSC fee card

Above: 1959-60 rally squad, Don in middle

Right: Heckart Lodge membership card

Far rght: Janet Essig's wrestling queen photo

This is to certify that

DON MOE ESSIG

is a member of

ZELIA HECKART LODGE

independent cooperative living organization

at

OREGON STATE COLLEGE

effective

1956

26

CHAPTER TWO

Going to Oregon State

*"The direction in which education starts a man
will determine his future life."*

—Plato
The Republic

There comes a time in every life when a life-altering decision has to be made. Don Duck, as he is now remembered by old time Beaver buddies and supposedly by his new found Duck dudes as well, was preparing to make his choice. Would it be Oregon State? Not good thinking, according to his Webfoot friends, but a good positive way to go as suggested by his Beaver believer pals.

What would persuade him which way to go? The actual decisionmaker turned out to be J. Thompson Prothro, the newly hired Beaver football coach from UCLA. Of course there was the positive feedback from cousin Bob, who was already enrolled on the Beaver campus. Much input came from his high school mates who were going to Corvallis. The crowning impetus came when Don and a group of his senior friends from Oregon City attended a Beaver football game in 1955 in Portland, Oregon's Multnomah Stadium.

Oregon State was a huge underdog to the Stanford Indians (later to be known as the Cardinal; the color not the bird). The previous year Prothro was an assistant at UCLA, a perennial football power in the old Pacific Coast Athletic Conference. At Oregon State he inherited a football team that had one win and nine losses in the past season.

The first time Oregon State had possession of the ball, the black clad Beavers came out of their huddle and serpentined to the line of scrimmage, as was the game habit of the UCLA Bruins! The Oregon State crowd went berserk! From that point on the cheering never stopped. Oregon State won the game and as Don later pointed out, "The place went absolutely nuts." This sequence of events he said was the biggie that prompted him into becoming a Beaver.

Don began spending more time on the Corvallis campus. Bob was a sophomore and other friends were already enrolled in the school. He came to Oregon State in the spring of 1956 and was accepted into Heckart Lodge, a men's cooperative living house on campus that cost about as much as it would have cost living in a campus dormitory. The lodge was owned by the college and could house only 60 male students, primarily from small Oregon towns whose families did not find it financially easy to send their sons off to college.

Don found it to be a comfortable transition from living at home. He said everything seemed to fall into place for him, "a good fit with a very close knit group of guys."

Heckart and other similar lodges were men's living groups thought of by many on campus as "poor kids" fraternities. Many African-American athletes at OSC chose these living arrangements as most satisfactory for them. They were not allowed access into fraternities because of the prevalence of discriminatory practices then occurring on college campuses around the country.

Being from a small farming community like Oregon City, Don had little experience dealing in minority situations. The give and take of this close communal living started Don on a lifelong acceptance of people of all races and faiths.

Responsibilities for living in a co-op included varying duties each resident had to do each week. Jobs such as setting tables, cleaning, doing the dishes and other such chores had to be shared by all the occupants.

Taking care of these obligations readily fit into the lifestyle of just about all those who lived in the lodge. They came from homes or farms where they had to pitch in and help their families. What it did for these young men included knowing the meaning of what it meant to help out in a community setting. It also helped to build a spirit of cooperation and teamwork. Camaraderie was manifest; the horsing around, the grab ass, the teasing, and the snapping of towels at one another's butts!

Other lodge functions parodied those in the fraternities; intra-mural sports, group exchanges with women's dorms and sorori-ties, and having house dances where the members had a chance to meet up with coeds on the campus and develop some good relationships. This was particularly true for the men of Heckart as many of their exchanges took place with the women of Sack-ett and its four all-girl dormitories, which were located directly across the street from where they lived.

Some of these parties with the "girls across the street" ended in "panty raids." It seemed the boys of Heckart after a party, would produce a stunning array of panties and bras which would end up hanging over the street between the two houses. This undergar-ment display greeted the early morning class-goers heading off to school from other campus residences or locales.

Of course, this didn't set too well with Helen Moore, Dean of Women at OSC. No one was caught participating in this nefarious college prank, even though it seemed to occur quite frequently. When Don was confronted and asked about this improper behav-ior, he pleaded innocence,

"I never became involved." Sure, and there's a 58,000 seat sta-dium in Eugene that he would like to sell to anyone who would believe him!

Don Essig's freshman year was definitely a growing up one for him.

He started off enrolling in Agricultural Engineering. It didn't work out. How he prepared himself in high school didn't fit in with the demands put on him in engineering school. He put considerable effort into the classes, but still went on academic probation, barely acquiring the first term grade point average that allowed him to stay in Heckart. He remembers the Dean of Engineering telling the new students in the program to look to the left and then to the right, and then he suggested that those two guys quite possibly won't be in engineering when it comes time to graduate. It undoubtedly was true enough, but Don said he only had to look in the mirror to figure he was going to be the odd man out. He did make it through two terms in Engineering.

Don came to the conclusion he had to have counseling to figure out which direction his life was going to take him. He went to the Counseling Center, took a battery of tests and found out that he was a people person. He didn't belong in Engineering but should look at something that was more people oriented.

Changing to a non-major spring term, he tried something that would exploit his people skills, one that would better fit into his personality. This differing attack on his education sounded great but another problem developed; his socializing became a bigger part of his college experience. Study and classes were beginning to take a back seat.

One of his first "socializing" experiences occurred at a home football game. Don never had much to do with alcoholic consumption in his life before college. Going to the second game of the year for the Beavers, he and a couple friends from Heckart had a few sips of wine before the game.

This made them feel so good that they sneaked a bottle of vino under Don's overcoat prior to entering the stadium to see the game.

It was raining "cats and dogs" in Parker Stadium, according to Don.

Before the opening kickoff to start the game, the future "Voice of the Ducks" stood up as if it weren't even raining in Parker Stadium to join the Beaver students in a cheer. Guess what? Out of his coat dropped the wine bottle which crashed to the concrete floor at his feet. It seemed as though the entire student body at the game stood up and pointed at Don and his pals.

They heckled, jibbed and jeered, as college students are prone to do.

Security back then was minimal, so Don and his drinking dudes were not apprehended and got to stay at the game. Don stalwartly proclaims he never again took an alcoholic beverage to an athletic event. Some wags agree that's easy for him to say, sitting way up there in the warm press box as he now does in Oregon's Autzen Stadium.

Just as his earliest affiliation with Beaver football started off with a big win over Stanford in Multnomah Stadium, Don's next big game encounter in his first year as an Oregon Stater would be the Beavers playing the Iowa Hawkeyes in the Rose Bowl on January 1,1957.

Don was now comfortably ensconced in the school's social life. He went to the Rose Bowl with cousin Bob and three of his house brothers.

Their down-coast journey was made all the more interesting by riding in a 1944 Hudson; bad tires, no freeways in Oregon, and massive fog in Ashland, Oregon, the trip had its other moments, but the payoff for Don was staying in Los Angeles in a Watts home of one of his Afro-American house brothers. Don says it was the highlight of the trip, one that he will never forget.

With all this happening his first year on the Beaver campus, what does the future portend for this "gonna-be" Duck?

Certainly one of the highlights in Don's time at Oregon State was meeting his future spouse, Janet Aune. She was a member of Alpha Chi Omega Sorority. The Alpha Chis were notorious for having some of the most attractive girls on campus in their house. Don became smitten by Janet and gave her a ride home for Thanksgiving the first year they met.

They began going steady Don's junior year, 1958.

An accomplishment for Janet was being selected by the Oregon State wrestlers to be one of their wrestling Queens. This story had its beginning with the Beavers highly successful wrestling coach, Dale Thomas. After his wrestlers placed well in the National Collegiate Wrestling Tournament, Coach Thomas was set to attend a national gathering of coaches to be held after the wrestling tournament. Before taking off for the meeting he was told by Oregon State Athletic Director, R.S. "Spec" Keene, "Do not" bring the national wrestling tournament to Corvallis!

Those who were closely acquainted with Dale Thomas knew not to even contemplate that idea with the irascible wrestling coach. After he mulled it over, sure enough, Dale, at the wrestling board meeting, laid out an offer to hold the wrestling tournament on the Beaver campus. The proposal was accepted by his national wrestling compatriots.

"What are they going to do to me," he was heard to ask, pertaining to the OSC Athletic Board's request? "Are they going to fire me for bringing a national tournament to Corvallis?" Nope. Concerned parties didn't think they could do that. Next year Corvallis would have itself a National Collegiate Wrestling Tournament, hosted by Oregon State College, thanks to Dale Thomas.

To help publicize the tournament, Dale came up with the idea of having wrestling Queens selected by OSC's wrestlers and named for the seven wrestling scores: Miss Takedown, Miss Escape, Miss Reversal, Miss Near Fall, Miss Fall, Miss Predicament and Miss Time Advantage.

Janet was named Miss Escape.

This notoriety, good or bad, brought instant fame to Oregon State through national newspaper outlets and magazines. Life magazine carried a photo of President August L. Strand walking through the campus. And, accompanying the picture, was the wrestling story. President Strand was leery of the publicity but eventually got caught up in the mood of the campus.

Pictures of the "Queens" were widespread. Janet confided that she had cards and letters from "people she didn't even know." She had a few proposals for dates and even a proposal of marriage!

Don got the message. He was being upstaged by some unknown letter writer and wrestling zealot. He and Janet were engaged spring term of his Senior year, and were married in June following his graduation in 1960.

When he became a sophomore, Don gave up his general studies and chose an elementary education major. One big difference he noted between Engineering and Elementary Education classes was that the ratio of boys to girls in engineering was about 2000 guys to 1 girl. In elementary education it was 6 guys to 300 girls! Go figure. Was changing majors that difficult a decision for a gregarious guy to make? What's a fella to do?

Don became much more motivated to go to class.

This was such a positive year for him he was able to buy his first car, of course with the help of Aunt Linda. She allowed him to pay $200 for her1949 Ford 2-door Deluxe. He didn't have to start paying her for it until graduation and he had his first teaching job. "It was a great car, and I still wish I had it today," he recently opined.

The summers of his sophomore, junior and senior years saw Don working for the Clackamas County paint and sign crew under the auspices of his father, Milton, who saw to the hiring of some 10 college students to help with the summer work. Another Heckart brother, Ron Rohweder, was teamed up with Don all three years to work on the paint crew. They were assigned a pickup truck for the painting and repair work. The money earned helped tremendously in offsetting college expenses. As Don recounted, "My parents didn't have an abundance of money so this summer working assignment made it much easier on them for me to go to school."

He pointed out that what he made came to about $1,000 each of the three summers he worked. When totaled out, his sophomore and junior year costs were less than the $1,000 allotted for the three terms of tuition and room and board.

Probably Don's most active year in college was as a junior. It started off by his being elected to the Beaver Bookstore Board of Directors. He became President of the Board as a senior. Another biggie, in an all-school election, he was chosen as the OSC Rally King for the eleven-member cheer leading team for 1959-60. Other men joining Don on the team were, Phil Estipular, Mike

McCuddy, Howie Smith and Don Wirth. The Coeds were Kathi Booth, Sally Elden, Ginny Evans, Janice Phillips, Judy Query and Gerry Rose.

Campaigning for the Rally King role, Don had fellow Heckart Lodge African-American brother, and All-American 250-pound football lineman, Ted Bates, pull him around campus in a little red wagon with taped-on signs that were attached to each side of the wagon: "Vote for Essig!" He was sure that was what won him the election.

That could very well be! In addition to Ted being a large, husky, twoway All-American lineman, he also was soft spoken, compassionate and well liked by Oregon State students. It was reported that on one occasion Ted was trying to incapacitate a frog by sticking a needle in the back of its neck in a science lab class. As his partner was doing the chore, Ted looked on, and passed out. So much for Beaver footballers who were "men of iron whose strength will never yield."

As a senior in 1959-60 there came many great memories. Don was selected Social Chairman for Heckart Lodge. This came right down his alley getting to arrange social events with women's dorms and sororities.

Throughout his Heckart years, except for his senior year when, loaded down with extracurricular activities, he also was actively involved in intramural football and basketball games, playing for Heckart.

Oregon State athletic programs became front and center for him during his senior year, in as much as his being head of the OSC rally squad. The football record, 3-7, for this year was the worst in Coach Tommy Prothro's entire football tenure at the Beaver school. The basketball team, headed by longtime coach A.T. "Slats" Gill, had a 50% won-lost record for the same year.

A fun time came when Rally went with the football team to a game at University of California. Coming from the cooler northwest the rally group wore sweaters. Temperature at game time in Cal Stadium was in the 90's!

The cheerleaders got cooked. What was known about the Beaver footballers was that they didn't "get cooked." They won the game!

Friends and acquaintances could be assured that the use of his voice in lecturing, recitations, public address speaking, or even Public Address announcing would have to be a defining make-up of any life story of Don Essig. While he was involved in many activities as part of his membership in Heckart Lodge, to him his big accomplishment was organizing and singing with "The Trends." He and two house brothers, Roy Rockhill and John Knaupp, formed the group and performed in many campus talent shows and at Heckart house functions. They also sang at some downtown restaurants in Corvallis.

Teaming up with Bob Richardson Don helped create, as well as develop along with an Oregon State Memorial Union leadership team, a "Fridays at 4" talent show. It took place every other week in the MU Ballroom and featured some very accomplished students in various acts and presentations. From the beginning, the Friday afternoon show enjoyed a packed audience. It was a popular venue because so many amateur individual and student groups were presented the opportunity to perform.

Don noted that another highlight in his musical life as a singing Beaver was his experience vocalizing with the OSC "College Choraliers," a singing group directed by music professor Bob Walls. There were many great trips with these vocalists and Don developed a number of new lifetime friendships along the way in this musical venture .

There were good-time stories with this group; very few bad. One person who sang with Don was Leo Holland. Through coincidence, Leo would end up marrying Janet's cousin while he was serving in the Army and stationed in Hawaii.

Another acquaintance who sang next to him with the choraliers was Mike Doherty, who is often identified by many knowledgeable sports fans as "the winningest high school basketball coach in Oregon." Don tells the story that later in his teaching career he was invited to a Doherty-coached game in Oregon City to be the game announcer for that night.

The least enjoyable venture from those singing years was a fish story that isn't really one of those exaggerated fish whoppers. On a singing trip to Coos Bay a family hosted a huge crab feed at their house for the choraliers after the concert. Everyone just pigged out on the crab.

In the middle of the night and not feeling too well, Don woke up and looked into the mirror. His face was all swollen and beet red! Not knowing what else to do he took two aspirin and went back to bed. The swelling eventually went down but the redness remained for quite a few days. From that day forward Don could not eat crab. He accepts the fact that they just keep being crabby with him. He insists that at that time crab was the only fish he couldn't eat. Later on in his life he discovered that lobster was another no-no and was put on his fish-allergy list.

To round out this final year of Don's OSC athletic experiences behooves one to go back to a February 12, 1987, sports column in the *Corvallis Gazette-Times*, written by sports editor Roy Gault. It was headlined, "Voice of the Ducks one-time OSU Prankster." Don told the following story to Roy. It goes without saying that he also related the same story to some Eugene friends.

Gault pointed out in his written piece that 1959 was "poor timing" for Essig as an OSC Rally King with football having a losing season and mens basketball going 13-13. As Gault's story unfolds, in 1959 the Beavers were big underdogs to the Ducks in the Civil War game to be held in Eugene.

Don relates, "A bunch of 'campus leaders' decided to fire up the team for the game." One of the students was the student body president; others included the president of Blue Key, senior men's honorary society; the editor of the OSC Barometer, student newspaper; the Rally King; a campus basketball hero who was also President of the Varsity "O" lettermen's club, plus others. It was an auspicious gathering of so called student "campus leaders."

This group ran off 5,000 pamphlets to spread around campus the day before the game denigrating the OSC football team. In addition, they procured a pickup truck, went to the pig barns just west of campus, bagged some manure, came back to Gill Coliseum and emptied the bags down the ramp leading to the Beavers' team locker room. The footballers would have to slog through the pig stuff to go out to practice in the stadium the day before the big game. Topping it off was a huge sign on the manure pile that read, "The Ducks Will Crap on the Beavers!"

The Barometer editor had a story posted in the paper the next day suggesting that the marauders were undoubtedly from the University of Oregon; "coming to ransack our campus and ridicule our football team."

The real home-grown BMOC pranksters got away with this in-house campus caper!

Essig told Gault, "I think it worked. We won the Eugene game, 15-7. If we had been caught pulling that prank we would have been kicked out of school."

Not told in the Gault story were events that occurred prior to and immediately following the game itself. The Oregon Ducks picked up some revenge. Female members of OSC's rally were "captured" by the Duck cheerleaders and were threatened to be passed up through the Oregon student section. Cooler heads prevailed and it didn't happen.

At the end of the game some raucous Oregon State students loudly let it be known, from their bleacher seats, which team had won!

Consequently, some rowdy Duck students picked up chunks of mud from the turf of old Hayward Field on the Oregon campus, grouped together in front of the Beaver student section, and started throwing clods of the stuff towards the Oregon State students. University police promptly broke up a soon-to-happen mele, but not before Rally King Don Essig was pelted in the back with a mud ball!

So it went with Beaver Don who was later to become Don Duck.

Following his senior year at Oregon State, the Beaver school became a University. He was in the final graduation class at Oregon State College. It was a busy year: rally practices, pep rallies, "Fridays at 4," singing with the choraliers and with "The Trends," emceeing a number of campus events (even the annual inter-fraternity sing, although he wasn't in a fraternity), and serving as president of the bookstore board of directors. He was busiest of all dating Janet full time.

During spring term of his final year, Don was scheduled to do his student teaching at Lincoln Elementary School in Corvallis. What better way to start off his teaching career than to have his supervising teacher become ill with an appendix episode. Bob Simonson had his wife become the certified substitute teacher, which effectively gave Don his first full-time teaching experience, even though he had not yet obtained his Oregon teaching certificate! As he pointed out, this full-time teaching in only his third week of student teaching prepared him well.

Don proudly pointed out that he closed out his Oregon State student career on a highly positive note. He graduated from the School of Education with two of his grandparents present for the ceremony: his mother's father, Edward Bittner, and his father's mother, Louise Essig, along with other members of the family. Upon graduation, Don was offered a full-time teaching assignment at Lincoln School but he had already signed a contract to return to his old home town, Oregon City.

Above: Son Scott at age 2, born in Portland. Don & Janet Wedding, 1960
Below: Don's first 6th grade class at Park Place School, 1960

CHAPTER THREE

Back to Oregon City

*"Children are the windows
through which we get to see the future."*

—Emily Wilson
6th grade teaching partner

Now it's on to home town school district, Oregon City. Don was well prepared for his first de-facto teaching experience. He contracted to teach fifth grade, the same grade in which he did his student teaching. Some subjects were not that much different from those he taught in Corvallis. He was sure the transition would be smooth.

After Don and Janet settled into their first home together in Oregon City, Don got the upsetting news that the person he was supposed to have replaced as 5th-grade teacher at Park Place School had decided not to retire and was now returning to the school. He was reassigned to a sixth grade class instead.

Now this presented a different ball game. Science classes were different from fifth grade, and the social studies program was totally geared toward Latin-America and Canada. Not to be deterred, Don received permission from Principal Clare Rasmussen to obtain the textbook and class materials he needed from the school and went home that summer to bone-up on those areas that he explained, "I didn't know beans about." He gathered up his personal fifth grade teaching accumulation and put it into storage, never to be used again.

Back in the 60's, teachers had only one day of paid planning; usually the day after Labor Day. Don Essig, always prepared to show as well as give his best, and wanting to impress the school staff, whom he had never met, spent Labor Day washing and polishing his brand new, old '49 Ford so it would "look great in the parking lot."

In as much as he was an early person, Don was the first into the grass-covered car parking area behind the school. He went directly up the stairs to his classroom. Mr. Rasmussen was the first to welcome him to the school and asked if that was his '49 Ford in the lot. "Yes, Sir," and he was waiting for the principal to give him a compliment on his great car. "Well, you better go move your car, because Emily Wilson has parked in the exact same spot for the past 34 years and she won't appreciate you being there!"

"Whoops!" Back down the three flights of stairs and out to the parking lot to move his car. This is not the first and certainly not the last of the disappointments Don would have to face up to in all his professional career. Even so, he still conjured up bad thoughts about Emily Wilson: probably overweight, stuck in her ways, just an old bag were some of the thoughts that bounced through his young, new to teaching, 21-year-old brain.

It wasn't long after this that Don got into his early-morning planning when he was greeted in his classroom by Emily Wilson. She was a bit overweight and considerably older, as he expected. He felt a bit confident in the premonition he had had of her; that was until she swooped across the room and gave him a big hug; this in a time when a veritable stranger would never give a hug in public. He was also taken aback when she said, "I am so damn glad to see you! I'm your sixth grade teaching partner!"

Emily continued winning over the spanking new teacher, "And, you play the piano?" Don nodded, yes. "Great! I hate teaching music. I hear you like sports and were involved in it in college?"

"Yep."

"Okay!" Emily concluded that they were going to make a great team at Park Place. She said she also hated teaching P.E. classes and asked, "What do you want to trade?"

Easy pickings for Don, "How about social studies and science?" It was a done deal. For the next three years Don taught both his and Emily's classes in P.E. and music. She never missed a class he taught, and she helped him in his classes in any way she could. He served as a kind of an assistant to her in the social studies and science classes she championed.

This experience with Emily turned out to be one of Don"s major learnings which would later be incorporated into his personal as well as professional life. He found out that Emily, although she may have been a little overweight and older, was in no way the pompous stick-in-the mud that he had envisioned. Don says he found out early not to judge people too soon before getting to know them. Following this advice can help a person to be successful and accomplish much in life. This was, without a doubt, the first time in his now blossoming career that Don learned, as he propounds, "perception is everything," but be careful not to create perceptions too early or before one gets all the facts to put them into reality.

From this experience a fact has to be assumed which is still not too well publicized in education that a seasoned 63-year-old and a neophyte 21-year-old can make a "pretty good teaching team". This happened before anything was written or tested out in education dealing with team teaching. Those three years with her flew by, and he says he will be forever grateful for the efforts and support that he always received from Emily Wilson. She played an influential role in his lifelong learning processes.

A little side note about Emily's knowledge of Don's ability is needed.

How did she ever know, or learn all that pre-teaching stuff about Don? The answer to this supplication is obvious in its probability. It was due to the influence of Mrs. Natalie Essig, Don's Mother! Emily and Natalie were members together of the Eastern Star organization in Oregon City. Natalie had pumped the matronly senior teacher full of information about how great her oldest son was! Emily took it from there.

This first year of teaching for Don even brought out more members of the Essig family as well as some recollections of working with his Dad during his Oregon State summers. Park Place School had an unmarked blacktopped playground on which the kids played during recess hours. A number of games were played in this area with the students themselves chalking in the lines for the respective activities in which they were participating. Papa Milton Essig was consulted about this game playing impropriety. Don and his Dad came over to the school on a Saturday morning with some bright yellow paint and painting equipment. They spent the day measuring and painting in game lines on the blacktop.

Come Monday one can only imagine the amazement and thrill the kids felt when they went out to play during recess! By far the most decorated playground with game lines in the city. It was also almost a godsend for the teaching staff in demonstrating the proper rules and procedures for Foursquare, Tetherball, Hopscotch, plus other made-up games. It not only helped in supervising play with rules being properly followed but it also led to far fewer arguments.

As an aftershock to Don and Milton's painting of the lines was that Don carried it over in his following years of teaching. Marked playgrounds were put in place at other schools where he was either a teacher or an administrator during the next 18 years: Willagillespie, Spring Creek, Francis Willard and Howard Elementary schools. It was just another unexpressed attitude of Don Essig; schools are not only places where lessons are taught, they are also where they are learned!

Sometimes a first-year teacher has difficulties dealing with discipline. Not so for Don. A large part of his classroom regimen dealt with humor.

Knowing that part of the students' diversion in classes was looking at the clock, watching the time fly by. Even the greatest of teachers had to faceup to that attention grabber. Why were the clocks positioned in the front of the room to make it easier for student viewing, but harder for teachers when lecturing their classes?

Don had a solution. He placed a printed poster above the front-wall timepiece that said, "Time Will Pass. Will You?" He attended the 40th year high school reunion of his first sixth-grade class. One of the attendees brought up the sign and wasn't bashful about pointing out it was one of the things she never forgot about Mr. Essig and his methods of teaching.

There were other issues of seeing, listening and learning. Don's class was directly across from the principal's office. He always kept his classroom door open, not only for ventilation or for a feeling of relief from being pent up but also for easy access to outside support. Don says he had another purpose. Back in those days in education the principal had a little more leeway in disciplinary procedures. In fact, Mr. Rasmussen had a "hack paddle" in his desk and on occasion would use it on a particularly unruly student. A loud groan or gasp would come across the hall from the Principal's office when a problem student was getting his "butt smacked."

One can imagine the effect these periodic outbursts from the front office had on Don's students! According to Don, none of his students had the desire to go across the hall to see Principal Rasmussen under similar circumstances. Don felt this situation made it more conducive to a proper learning atmosphere in his classroom.

The socioeconomic factor of Park Place was diverse: close to half of the student body came from the more affluent side of town where the families had most of the finer things in life and lived pretty comfortably. The other side of town had 50% of the students coming from a county welfare project that was located about six blocks from the school. These were houses provided for families with very little or no income whatsoever. Most of these kids were seldom fortunate enough to be able to go home to a clean house and a balanced meal, if they had much to eat at all.

Don was quite impressed very early in his first year of teaching that, at least in his classes, there would never be any difference, except with the way the students dressed: not in behavior or in their willingness to assist one another. It was an insistence on tolerance that Park Place had. All the students were treated the same regardless of backgrounds or economic status. Don's personal learning curve was continually expanding in his dealing with such a diverse population of elementary aged young people.

Summer of 1961 came to Park Place and the Essigs, along with their recently born son, Scott, returned to Corvallis and Oregon State University.

Janet was completing her classwork for a Bachelor's Degree in Elementary Education. Don was picking up his first experience in retail sales. He was given a swing shift job at the 29th Street Superette Market on Harrison, just across the street from the Oregon State campus. He'll tell you it was just another great learning experience.

He'd see large families with super large charge accounts, some who could hardly make a complete payment each month. Then there were those who allowed their young children to put a lone popsicle on their family account. This required filling out a charge slip for a mere nickel!

Some of the youngsters would walk out the door throwing the paper wrapper and the charge slips on the floor! Maybe a bit spoiled? This wouldn't ever be acceptable in a Don Essig classroom!

Because of the swing shift, this summer plunged Don into yet another future new experience--golf. When he was off work he and another close friend from Oregon State days, Scott Rickard, who also was on swing shift at a local lumber mill, teamed up for golf. They signed in at the Albany Golf Club course for $10 a month to play all the golf they could handle. They became fairly good at the game, and it became Don's new enduring athletic activity.

Through the years he picked up a six handicap. Then something happened. Age sneaked up on him and so did his handicap. Today he will admit that golf is not only for exercise, but also a great way to create new friendships. If bad shots or high scores don't interfere with your vision, it also is a great way to enjoy nature; so Don says. Don enjoyed those golfing days with Scott, who, not so incidentally, was the namesake for Janet and Don's first-born son.

Don began work on his Master's Degree in school administration at Portland State College in Portland, taking both night and summer classes.

To get into graduate school Don had to first take and pass 18 hours of graduate credit to prove he could handle the graduate program. His undergraduate studies left something to be desired, they didn't shine too brightly at Oregon State. He admits to too much partying and fun with the guys. So, here's another new ballgame. Now he had a spouse and son to hook up to his desire and motivation to succeed. He cleared this scholastic hurdle with all A's and B's.

To go along with Don meeting the requirements for admission to a graduate program, in the fall of 1962 he was approached by a representative of the Oregon City High School booster club about public address announcing for the boys' basketball team. He was told that he had a great voice, and was asked if he was interested. Don checked in with Dan Jones, Oregon City High School Athletic Director to get the appointment cleared. Don already knew Dan as they had officiated high school football games together the previous year. It was a go.

Don became the school's announcer.

In a Park Place School hallway meeting, a career of announcing athletic events for high school, college and even some semi-pro games was born.

Spring of 1963 brought the opportunity as well as the desire to move to Eugene to complete his Masters program. It was not possible to get an administration degree at Oregon State. The former Oregon State Beaver yell King was going to become a Duck. He obtained a teaching position in the Eugene School District for the fall and entered summer school at the University of Oregon.

The hardest part of this move came when he had to tell Emily Wilson that he was leaving Oregon City and moving to Eugene. Emily broke down and cried and told him how much she would miss working with him. Don felt in his heart how important his first three years were working with Emily, and what it had meant to him. He says he has never forgotten and will always remember and appreciate the many lessons she had taught him.

Above: Masters degree with Janet, 1964. Son Ted at two, born in Eugene

Above: PhD with Janet, Scott, Ted and with parents Milton & Natalie, 1971

Right: First Eugene home, bought in 1967

CHAPTER FOUR

On to Eugene

"When you're through changing,
you're through."

—Bruce Barton
Philosopher

Come September, 1963, right after school was out in June, the North American Van & Storage truck backed up to Don, Janet and Scott's apartment in Oregon City, loaded up the furniture and off the family headed for a brand new adventure awaiting them in Webfoot City.

January, 1963, Don attended a Portland conference geared toward teachers and administrators. One of the presenters, Mrs. Vera Moomaw, was there with teachers from the Eugene School District who were titled as Resource Teachers. They each went to an elementary school, but none were assigned to a classroom. They worked with gifted kids in math and language arts. Don attended the workshop and afterwards had a long chat with Vera concerning the District and his chances of landing a teaching job in Eugene. Vera was impressed with his music credentials and his willingness to work with any grade level.

As a result of this conversation Don called the Eugene personnel office, completed the application form and set up a meeting with Personnel Director Warner Kirlin. Not withstanding lost application papers Mr. Kirlin, was in a cast from falling and breaking a leg. Considering the Director was also being somewhat vague during the interview, the discussions went very well. When Don opened up about his music abilities and his experience teaching and directing elementary choir, Mr. Kirlin came alive. Classroom teaching, as well as music instruction became Don's forte. As they might say in Ireland, Don Essig "was in like Flynn!"

In about two weeks the letter came in that he would be teaching sixth grade at Willagillespie School in Eugene! Of course he had to begin practicing pronouncing the name. He found out the name came from the Gillespie family, donors of the property for the school, and from the nearby flowing Willamette River. Thus the name, Willagillespie, was created.

Okay. A place to teach. How about a place to live? Later he would get into the University's graduate program. The Eugene Essigs were fortunate because coming to the rescue were old friends from their Oregon State days. Heckart Lodge roommate Ken Ramsing, and his wife, Margo, put them up (or maybe even put up with them) for a short time until Janet discovered an ad in *The Eugene Register-Guard* newspaper of a duplex in west Eugene for an affordable $100 a month. They grabbed it, paid Mr. Harvey the rent, and made their move in June. No one knows for sure how the Ramsings felt about losing their tenants. It had to be a feeling of relief for Don, Janet and Scott to leave and find their own space. It also had to be a good feeling for Ken and Margo, helping out friends and a former fellow Beaver classmate.

Don began his graduate program by securing the services of Dr. Dick Schminke, a professor of education. Dr. Schminke had Saturday duty in the department. This was a godsend for Don as it fit with his elementary class teaching schedule. Schminke was not only a mentor for Don's Master's program, but he carried on as the major advisor for Don's doctorate. It didn't stop here. He went on to become one of Don and Janet's closest friends.

Don's school, Willagillespie, seemed, to him, to be way out in the "boonies." Don and Janet looked the situation over and decided, together, they had made the right decision. They didn't particularly relish the idea of moving away from both sets of parents, but it was a job and they had to move on in the next phase of their unfolding lives. They were satisfied with the positive decision they made. It was a gutsy gamble for a young couple but one they were willing to make together.

After getting settled into their new home in June, Don signed up for and started into his summer graduate program. Getting to meet and know new people is a signature asset of Don's modus operandi. During registration for his graduate program he met Lon Kellenberger, a fellow teacher who was still teaching and living in Salem. He commuted each day to Eugene to take the summer classes. The two elementary teachers had a lot in common, each married to an elementary teacher and both had a young child, and they were each pursuing advanced degrees in curriculum and instruction.

Don and Lon had signed up for two classes together. One of the more notable classes turned out to be almost insufferable. It was a philosophy of education memorization hour. As Don pointed out, the entire class procedure involved reading books and rote learning statements from the assignment and regurgitating what they had memorized on tests the following Thursday. The most they said they had taken from the class was how not to teach their own students. Kellenberger turned out, for Don, to be "an enduring and very close friend."

Other friends of Don and Janet from Oregon City days, Tom and Nancy Keele, also moved to Eugene that summer of 1963. He was named the head football coach at the newly opened Sheldon High School. This meeting of old acquaintances led to another major adventure in the experiences of Don Essig. Through Tom, Don met Mel Krause, athletic director at Sheldon. Krause was a former outstanding Duck basketball and baseball player. He learned about Don doing the announcing at basketball games in Oregon City, and wanted him to do the games at Sheldon. It became another close bonding for the Essigs with the Krauses. Don would become indebted to Mel Krause for his public address announcing career.

The summer of 1964 saw new excitement for the family; son Ted was born in July. Father Don received his Masters degree in August. He was teaching sixth grade and was introduced to the very popular athletic activity, at least in Eugene, of track and field competition. Willagillespie was filled with track and field events for all grade levels and Don was steered into the program.

Another assignment foisted on him by Principal Don Eckenrode was being the building supervisor Monday nights when ladies of the community held their weekly ceramic class. This gave him a quiet night, a place to study, and a few extra dollars in the pocket. He had access to a typewriter and many school materials to use as references to help him pass his time productively.

The Essigs were well ensconced in the Eugene community and decided they would make the Webfoot city their permanent home rather than seeking jobs in another district or of returning to Oregon City. Janet was now staying home with her boys as a stay-at-home mom.

About this time a feeble little rain cloud began to appear over the Essig parade. It was in the form of Vera Moomaw, from the Portland Conference days, to interrupt Don's now well-planned-out life. She visited his classroom and observed his teaching. Another visitor was Dr. Evelyn Piper, Director of Elementary Education for the Eugene District. She came to watch him teach. Why these intrusions?

Vera and Principal Don Eckenrode met with Don about the possibility of his moving to the newly opened Spring Creek School as the school's resource teacher. This caused Don some consternation as to whether he wanted to leave Willagillespie after only one year.

Eckenrode encouraged him to go, not because he wanted him to leave, but because it posed a long-term benefit for his career. It would give him the opportunity to work with an entire staff and student body which would help him prepare for someday becoming a school Principal. Together he and Janet decided this would be a positive step forward in his career.

So, Don said goodbye to Willagillespie.

Spring Creek School was a new building with 12 classrooms and an all new staff. Principal Russ Tompkins, also had a brand new resource teacher. Don's assignment was to teach music and physical education to all 300-plus students. He was to supervise the lunchroom and picked up playground duty to keep him busy with his free time. Without doubt, his teaching day was filled up.

Russ was a devout Baptist and he supposedly had nothing to do with alcoholic beverages or smoking, so the whispered allegations suggested.

He also avoided the use of profanity. He always wore a suit and tie to school. Misgivings about the principal were rampant. Don had already learned about making quick decisions regarding people.

So what was the real skinny on Principal Tompkins? The rumors didn't stack up. He turned out to be as big a surprise to Don as he was to the rest of the school's personnel! At his first full staff meeting, Russ walked into a room choked with cigarette smoke. He hadn't realized the new staff he had taken on were mostly smokers, which included Don. The principal never said a word about it. In fact, there were always ash trays available in the staff lounge. However, all future staff meetings were held in the library, where no smoking was permitted!

Russ wore a suit and tie to school but never required the two male teachers to do the same. Although a strong Christian man, he never discussed it with staff nor did he make reference to others' religious beliefs or preferences. When he and his wife, Arlene, invited the staff to their home for a big spaghetti and tossed salad dinner, he was asked by a staff member what kind of wine to bring. He responded that he didn't know much about wine so bring whatever kind they wanted. This put a solid kibosh on the anti-drinking rumor. After that misconception came out just about every staff member brought wine of one kind or another. Oh, and it came out that, although Russ didn't drink alcoholic beverages himself, Arlene did like her glass of vino.

Just one of the many compliments Don would lay on Russ was his pronounced and proud patriotism. Every class at Spring Creek was required, every day, to stand, place their hand over their heart and recite the Pledge of Allegiance to our great country. For many years Russ taught citizenship classes to immigrants. Through his efforts and teaching, many people from all areas of the world became proud United States citizens.

Right: Don's announcing book, 1988

Below: Don in original Autzen press box, 1968

Right: Don with spotters Stan and Jack, 1982, UO against Notre Dame

CHAPTER FIVE

Public Address Announcing

"When opportunity knocks, some people are in the backyard looking for four-leaf clovers."

—Anonymous

During his second week of teaching at Spring Creek school, Don got a phone call from Mel Krause telling him that a new sound system was being installed in Civic Stadium and Sheldon would be playing a football game there this coming Friday night.

"Get your ass down there and announce the game!"

OK, come Friday night Don's buttocks were snugly seated in the press box to announce his very first football game! Mel said he would have some students there to help him with spotting. What a beginning for him and he would continue announcing for Sheldon High School until 1967.

Don had many positive experiences at Spring Creek. There were opportunities to work with dissimilar levels of students. He also got to work with varying staff members. He remembered many vignettes sitting down and chatting with Russ on a score of various teaching issues. The principal told him he wanted to give him as many tips as he could to help him get ready for that day when Don himself would become a principal.

Don was boastful about putting together a school-wide track and field program at Spring Creek, a feeder school for North Eugene High School.

The coaches at North were also proud of Don's efforts because track and field was a major sport at that school. They anticipated many talented track kids coming to North to compete.

Don was again grateful to another great mentor and idol for all the good preparation and training he had received from Russ Tompkins.

In the spring of 1966, Don found out that his former principal at Willagillespie, Don Eckenrode, had been transferred to Frances Willard School and wanted him back. With some consternation, he went with the plan. Another up-and-coming principal gonna-be, Mike Brott, took Don's place at Spring Creek. Mike also placed Russ Tompkins high on his list of favorite principal mentors.

The switch to Willard was almost anti-climatic. It is kind of ironic that Don was a first-grade student in the old Willard school on thirteenth Street before it burned down in 1954. Now he would be teaching in the newer building that was opened in 1955.

Vera Moonaw, who had helped Don get the job at Spring Creek, resurfaced in his teaching career and asked him to assist her in summer workshops. They would be writing curriculum booklets for elementary teachers in mathematic classes. This certainly would help out with family income. Janet was not teaching, and for the active life they were leading they were just getting by on Don's lone teaching salary.

Don's teaching at Willard included working with all the school's 450 students. The school had the largest gymnasium of any elementary school in the Eugene district. Each of his physical education classes often had between 60 to 75 students. The Hootenanny rage was spreading throughout the country and Don picked up on it at Willard on Friday afternoons. All the students in the school would go to the multipurpose room for an all-student-singalong. Sometimes different grade level groups would perform for the rest of the school.

At this time another unforeseen public address announcing job raised its not-so-ugly head. This time it was for the Eugene Bombers semi professional football team. The Bombers were made up of former Oregon State and University of Oregon football players. The games were played Sunday afternoons at the old Bethel Park. Often as many as 5,000 football adherents would show up to drink beer and watch the old timers, some of whom were overweight, many out of shape, and trying to mutilate one another out on the gridiron like they did, back in the days of yore. They did their best with whatever skills they had left.

The first year Don used his old Beaver buddy (me) to come down and spot for him. The two Orange pitchmen were perched in a makeshift press box (for lack of a better name) built over two of the stadium bleachers with a table of sorts for laying out their working papers.

When Don and Charlie Beaver showed up to work the games, there would be a six-pack of beer awaiting them on the table. Suffice it to say, that was their pay for the afternoon effort. However, they never partook of the beverages in order as to not disrupt their spotting and good field judgement. There also was a bigger problem. Bethel Park had a single men's restroom to accommodate all the men beer guzzlers! Don supposed there must have been something there for the ladies, too. The lines to the makeshift sheds were long ones.

Be that as it may, the Bomber games were fun and it gave valuable experience to Don in his announcing of football games.

That football fall, Don also became involved as a spotter for longtime and highly respected Oregon State sports PA announcer, Ted Carlson. At his alma mater, he gained new expertise and picked up differing insights into announcing the college game. He observed and took with him many of Ted's announcing techniques and strengths. Don later incorporated these into his own announcing.

Fall weekends were busy announcing two high school football games at Autzen Stadium in Eugene on Friday nights, and spotting for Carlson at Oregon State's Parker Stadium in Corvallis on Saturday. Come Sunday, there was choir at the Congregational Church in the morning, then off to Bethel Park and announcing the Bombers game in the afternoon.

Adding to his scheduled teaching and announcing gigs, he was on the the Board of Directors for the Eugene Education Association, local organization of teachers and administrators. Even the onset of winter didn't offset the demanding schedule very much. Basketball announcing at Sheldon High School just added to the full agenda of activities.

With the coming of spring in 1967, the duplex the Essigs lived in became smaller with the two boys, Scott and Ted, growing older and bigger; stuff was accumulating. A move had to be made. Don and Janet decided to buy their first home, even though Don didn't think they had enough money at the time. Later he found out that he had enough money in an insurance policy to allow them to make a down payment on a home and move out of the duplex.

On Independence day, July 4, some teaching friends showed up at the Essigs. They all pitched in and loaded a U-haul truck, and they were off to Birchwood Avenue in the Sheldon School area. They lived in this house for eleven years before they again felt a need for expansion Their sons were both becoming a lot more active, as were Mom and Dad. They moved again, ten houses down Birchwood in 1978, to a bigger home. All in all, they now have lived in the same neighborhood for over 44 years! Don continued helping in the workshops that summer and attended a three week-social studies institute in Ashland, Oregon, which gave him some additional graduate credit.

When school started in September, Don got a call from Johnnie Eggers, Sports Information Director at Oregon State, telling him that he no longer would be a spotter for Ted Carlson. Instead, he was going to be the inside-the-press-box game announcer for the Beavers. In this capacity he would be giving out official information to the press corps in the press box.

Once again, his old Beaver buddy, who worked with him back at the Bomber games, spotted for him in one of Oregon State's great all-time football games. Coach Dee Andros' "Giant Killers" Beavers knocked off the heavily favored Southern California Trojans, 3-0. Don could have said for that game, "It never rains in Parker!" Still, somehow, the field was a quagmire of mud from previous rains--at both ends of the field!

"Muddiest field ever," complained the sports writers from Southern California. It served as another great learning experience for neophyte public address announcer Don Essig.

The first day of November, 1967, was a day like all days except for Don. It became one of the biggies of his life! He received a phone call from Mel Krause, who had been at an Oregon Duck Club sports luncheon and had heard that Virgil Parker, the University's public address announcer, was moving to Nebraska. He told Don the announcing job was open and available. Again Mel's admonishment came over the wire, "Get your ass over to the athletic department!" Mel had already set up a 3:30 p.m. appointment for Don with Duck Athletic Director Norv Ritchey to talk about the public address announcing job.

Three different men were selected to each announce three different basketball games. Don was one of them. When the third game had finished Don received the call from Ritchey telling him they wanted him to be the Duck announcer for football, basketball and track.

And so it came to pass the former Oregon State Rally King, high school, Eugene Bomber and Oregon State announcer would hang up all of his orange and black memorabilia and switch to the green and yellow of the Oregon Ducks!

It was a great ride to this point and it even got better. This was the beginning of the era of Don Essig, public address "Voice of the Ducks."

Quite a journey for a 28-year-old whose life seems to have always been and continues to be in the positive thinking mode--if it can be done, then it will be done!

Each year seemed to become busier for Don: President of EEA, teaching full time, announcing high school games on Friday nights, announcing Duck basketball games plus his continued singing in the church choir. The family was settling into a different home, getting to know the new neighbors and learning to find their way around town from a different location. With only one car in the family, Don shared driving to Willard school with Dave Campbell who lived in the same neighborhood and who was an intern supervisor at Don's school, thus giving Janet use of the car for her journeys, for at least half of the week.

September 28, 1968, saw an inauspicious beginning for Don behind the mike at Autzen Stadium. The sky was clear with no rain in sight and the fans were hopeful, but the team didn't quite follow the future game plan in trying to help him clear this first announcing hurdle in Don's Oregon Duck football announcing career. Stanford University prevailed over the Webfoots, 28-12. It would take a few more years down the line and a whole lot more games for the mystique, "It never rains in Autzen," to come to fruition for Don and the university's enthusiastic football backers.

This first game for Don was also the first for one of his best friends, Jack Pynes, one of his game spotters. Jack has continued in that role, missing only two games for all of their years in the football press box.

Continuing the Friday night high school games, he occasionally worked a junior-varsity game that the University would have on Silke Field in Springfield on Saturday mornings. This before the varsity games at Autzen in the afternoon. To help him keep his weekend sanity, the Eugene Bombers closed their football franchise thus freeing up Don's Sunday afternoons.

Sometimes it seems that all this public address announcing would take over Don's primary mission in life, working, supporting and taking care of his family. All the extracurricular activities, including sports, wasn't putting that much bacon on the table. It seemed almost problematic that Lon Kellenberger, from Don's Masters degree program days, would call with an offer that unveiled something worth looking into. Lon was into a Doctoral program and wanted Don to take a beginning statistic class on Saturday mornings with him during winter term.

Don wasn't really interested in starting up another three-year graduate program. However, he did telephone and talk to his advisor, Dick Schminke, and was told that all of his credits on his Masters would count toward a doctorate. This would shorten his program by over a year of course work!

As if he didn't have anything else to do on Saturdays, he agreed to take the Saturday morning classes with Lon. Thinking positively, this statistics class was again loading up his activities schedule including announcing Duck basketball games on Saturday nights. However, it also was an opportunity to pursue a doctorate, something he hadn't much thought about before. Yep, he decided he'd go for it.

As the school year continued at Willard teaching remained pretty much the same. Don had a second term of statistics along with an elementary math seminar spring term giving him nine new hours of doctorate credits. This year also included his second year of announcing basketball games throughout the winter for the Ducks.

Right: Organization Development training group, 1972

THE EFFECTS OF A MULTI-UNIT, DIFFERENTIATED
STAFFING ORGANIZATION UPON TEACHERS'
ATTITUDES AND INSTRUCTIONAL PROGRAMS

by

DON MOE ESSIG

A DISSERTATION

Presented to the Department of Curriculum and Instruction,
the College of Education, and the Graduate School of the
University of Oregon in partial fulfillment of the
requirements for the degree of
Doctor of Philosophy

September, 1971

Above: Don's favorite Olympia typewriter and his dissertation title page, 1971

Right: Office in UO CASEA building, 1972

CHAPTER SIX

Organization Development Project

*"Courage is being scared to death,
and saddling up anyway."*

—John Wayne
Famous Actor

In the spring of 1969 a new, positive change of direction spurred Don's interest during this school year. Eugene's Superintendent of Schools, Millard Pond, wanted to institute a Differentiated Staffing Project into the school district. Don and Dick Arends were asked to coordinate and administer the project. As it turned out, it was an ideal situation for both of them. They could go to school full-time, work on their doctorates and still continue to work half-time for the district. They both would receive halftime pay and an office in the school district with all the services available to them for working as well as going to school. They accepted the superintendent's offer.

At the same time this was going on, the University of Oregon had an Organization Development Project of their own in progress. It was led by Richard Schmuck and Phil Runkel who were looking for some schools of their own for the project. So, along with Don and Arends, joint staffing and training was given birth. Another perfect match, as the power of positive thinking would describe it. Don and his partner had full access to 50 district schools and became coworkers with the Schmuck and partner team from the U of O. At the time neither Don or Dick knew that the university's OD project would become a major part of their doctoral programs.

With this new opportunity for Don off and running, Janet decided she wanted to put in her two cents worth. She began substitute teaching. Both Scott and Ted were full-time students: Scott in elementary and Ted in preschool. Janet's substituting had her teaching at Spring Creek School, Don's old stomping grounds. With Janet's new career off and running, the Essig income was at least matching what Don had been making as a fulltime teacher.

The summer brought more school for Don, both as a doctoral student and with a new professional position. The family settled into their new home. They even found finances to buy a second car. One thing was for sure with this family, the moss just never seemed to get a chance to grow under their feet.

Everything seemed to be neatly falling into place at home as Don was moving into a very different professional experience. For the first time in nine years he would not be teaching kids in an elementary school. The combination of working on a doctorate, coordinating the district with the University of Oregon Organization Development program, and attending graduate classes made for a new and different daily work schedule. Throw in public address announcing at UO athletic events and it made Don Duck a very busy person.

Working on the OD program with Dick Arends was another new experience merging two different teaching backgrounds: Don's in elementary education and Dick's at the high school level. It made for an ideal relationship. Both personalities meshed, and the proximity of their two shared offices in the district and at the University rounded out a warm team-working relationship. As the year progressed it became most evident that they thought alike, shared positive communication skills, and in general had similar working habits.

Don was introduced to an entirely new focus in communications, decision making, team building and innovative thinking from the University of Oregon's Differentiated Staffing/Organization Development project.

These agendas became the base for Don's later consulting business. They also played a major role in the rest of his professional career working in educational leadership.

The effective and very capable, as well as professional staff, were positive models for him later in his profession as a motivational speaker as well as a consultant in his Essig and Associates Consulting business.

According to Don, as the three years of the project progressed it became obvious that the OD project was on the right track in training teaching staffs to improve communications and become more cooperative in their working relationships. They also became more innovative in the thinking and the trying out of new and different ways of doing things.

"The data we received from the six initial school staffs was most valuable in expanding the results of the survey to other schools in the district," Don pointed out.

One of the major results was the creation of a communication cadre in the Eugene school district training other school staffs in the same basic skills as the original schools in the DS/OD project. The cadre continued for many years after the initial project was completed.

In August, 1971 Don completed all his work and received his PhD. He continued half-time with the school district and the OD staff. He began to spend more time working directly with the elementary school principals as the Cadre work expanded into other schools. This work continued throughout the 1971-72 school year.

All-in-all, it came time for Don Essig to start taking up a full-time work-a-day professional load. He let it be known to many or his friends and coworkers, as well as to other school districts and universities alike, that he was going to put into practice all the learning and experience he had acquired over the past three years.

To start the ball rolling for him in this new endeavor was an invite he received from Drake University in Des Moines, Iowa. They wanted him to come and be interviewed for a position that would coordinate student teachers from Drake into and with the Des Moines school district.

He went for it. The interview was a success, although, according to Don, it was somewhat different from those to which he had become accustomed. He said he sat in a circle with some 20 staff members from the district and from the university. They asked questions and then checked out Don's personality along with the answers he gave to their questions.

Don left Des Moines the following morning with a commitment from the Director of the program for which he was aspiring, that he would be recommending him for the position.

On the flight back home Don spent his flying time thinking about the proposition. Truth be told, he had some misgivings about leaving Eugene.

The Emerald City had become his family's home. He had accumulated a passel of friends in Webfoot town. A new move could also mean the end of his now emerging and popular public address announcing career.

As Don says, most of his cogitating on the plane ride home was for naught. He knew his strong working relationship with Roy Rutter, Director of the North Eugene regional schools, paid off for him when Roy met him at the Eugene airport with a school district contract in hand.

Confronting Don, Roy said, "You aren't going anywhere else. I need a principal at Howard Elementary School and you're it! Sign the papers and call the people back in Iowa and tell them you're not leaving Eugene."

Roy was so convincing in his presentation that Don didn't seek anyone else's advice, including Janet's. He just went ahead and signed the documents.

Thus began another road to follow: elementary school administrator with a building staff and kids. As it turned out, the conditions at Howard School were a perfect fit for Don's training and background in the project with the Eugene School District and the University of Oregon.

What Don learned was that there was a bit of animosity at Howard between the administration and staff. The ongoing criticism of the outgoing principal was that he did not present a very positive outlook in his administrative procedures which is a Don Essig priority! Communications within the staff was mostly nonexistent (this certainly would come to fruition in Don's scheme of leadership). As a result, there appeared to be much mistrust toward the outgoing administration, with little or no motivation at the school to innovate or change anything.

As far as Don was concerned, working together, making joint observations, and developing philosophies and values is "fundamental to what we call life." He recalled his initial meeting as a first year teacher with Emily Wilson at Park Place School in Oregon City. His preconceived idea of what she was like was way offside and he promised himself he would try hard to not let that happen again.

Writing in the Food Service Journal in 1992, Don wrote an article titled: "Seeing Both Sides: Key to Leadership Success." He wrote out, "When we first meet someone we're introduced to a quick 5 percent: appearance, face, hair, tone of voice, clothes. It takes some effort to find the other 95 percent of the person." This he says is what leadership is all about.

This was Don's opportunity to find out if all the concepts he had learned and taught throughout the project would pan out when he became the school's formal leader.

71

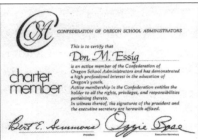

Above: Howard Elementary School picture, 1974 and his Oregon School Administrators' certificate

Right: Howard phone book fiasco, 1975

CHAPTER SEVEN

Howard Elementary School

*"I never did a day's work in my life—
It was all fun."*

—Thomas Edison
Master Inventor

Don's first principalship at Howard Elementary School began in the spring of 1972 before the school year had ended. The previous principal had already been transferred to another school. This put the new Howard principal into his office and on the job even though the contract didn't begin until July.

As events occurred and difficult situations came up during Don's six-year leadership, how he worked with and through these sometimes difficult situations, it's easy to see why Don often referred to his tenure at Howard as a major highlight of his professional career. His advocacy for both teachers and students presented opportunities to control the educational aspirations of both learner and instructor to better obtain the maximum results for both.

When Don entered Howard for the very first time, the initial staff member he met was Edith Traynor, the school secretary. Upon introducing himself to her the very first thing she said to

73

him was, "Are you going to keep me?"

After accepting his appointment, Don spent some time researching the school and its staff. What he had already learned about Edith was that she had been at the school for over 20 years. He further found out that she was one of those trying to hold the staff together during the difficult times.

Don's response to Edith's question: "What I found out about you, Edith, is if I don't keep you, I'm dead!"

Her smile immediately indicated, and proved true, that this was to be an exemplary principal-secretary relationship for the next six years. Edith's initial information to Don was invaluable in his first communications and planning with the entire staff. A lasting component of this close relationship happened in April, 2012 when Edith had Don as her guest at a luncheon in her honor celebrating her 96th birthday!

It didn't take long to determine he was ensconced with some very competent teachers. He was sure that they would comfortably fit themselves into a leadership team arrangement designed for the Differentiated Staffing Project that he had helped bring into the schools.

His plan called for a teacher team-leader for each two grade levels, plus an extra week of planning in the fall for the school staff. Instead of every two grade levels, the staff opted for a team leader for each grade level. This meant Don had to hunker down and plead with Roy Rutter for an extra week of work for seven people instead of four.

One of the techniques Don used was to have each team make two lists: "What's working?" and "What can be improved?" Posted on selected walls in the school, it enabled teams to forge an overall plan of education for the school and staff beginning in the upcoming school year.

Another vexing problem facing the new school principal was what to do with the staff's lounge which was located directly behind and adjoining the principal's office. This seemed like a minor decision, but many of the staff wanted to be out of the way and in a more relaxed atmosphere where their comments to one another would not be misinterpreted or judged as gossip by the principal or other office members. According to the staff, the former principal wanted the lounge to be close at hand so he could quell any rumors or hearsay. Don felt the lounge should be a place of downtime relaxation. It was a good move for creating a cooperative and positive working relationship with the school members.

In his principal role at Howard he hired a new guidance counselor. Janet Skuce was not only an outstanding guide and confidant for the young people now in her care, she also was most helpful in a similar role for Don and the staff. She proved to be most proficient in dealing with kids' unacceptable behavior and aiding and abetting them through many of their personal problems. Janet was also a great asset in helping Don better understand how to utilize logical consequences in problems that arose with the staff, as well as with the students.

Janet was a participating member of the school district's Communication Cadre that Don helped develop. Without a doubt, this close relationship with Jan had to help him in his growth as an administrator.

There were some fun things that could be done at Howard. Don took the cue to produce and incorporate what he had panned out and accomplished as a teacher at other schools. The sense of humor of both he and his staff could certainly make this a fun place to work and learn.

The grade-level teams got busy brain storming activities that could be organized and completed with the primary end-result being that Howard School provided a positive learning experience as well as a "fun place" to be; every day!

All-school talent shows became regular events for staff and students. The school mascot became the "Roadrunner".

Add in Friday afternoon sing-alongs for all 450 students. Yes, Don was sometimes at the piano keyboard. It was like going back to his early teaching days at Park Place School in Oregon City. Don's dad, Milton, even pitched in again by bringing his painting equipment from the farm in Oregon City to doll up Howard's school yard with a variety of lines for different games and activities which were organized with kids in mind.

Differing rewards were laid out for all who participated. There were no losers, everyone was made to feel like a winner.

Another big payoff for Principal Don, who often pulled playground duty freeing up teachers for lunch, was playing 4-Square Ball with the kids.

He really liked the game and thought he was fairly good at it. The daily "Put the Principal Out in 4-Square" became popular, and anyone that could put him out of the square received a certificate acknowledging the nefarious deed. The lines of those wanting to play the game became long as the students awaited their chance to take on the "The Man", and try to get the paper testimony to verify that they had indeed put "the Principal out", and they would have the verification for friends and family to show what they had accomplished.

When asked why he spent so much time on the playground, he responded, "When the principal (almost like a God to the kids) is on the playground, kids don't throw rocks, don't kick balls up on the roof, don't say naughty words and don't argue with and hit each other. When "God" is not on the playground he's going to spend a couple of hours after lunch dealing with the kids who did all those things when he wasn't there!"

Don had become so absorbed in playing with the kids on the playground he admitted later that he hasn't attained such great measure of physical shape ever since leaving Howard!

Nicknames became a game with Don in his relationships with his young charges. These nicknames were most commonly related to their actual names. It stands to reason that the young people would create a name for him.

How about "Egghead"? To the students he was the top teacher as the principal and it came fairly close to "Essig." Don felt highly honored by the many "Mr. Egghead" pictures drawn by the students that later adorned his office walls.

Don tells the story that at one of the parent night programs, a first grader was walking down the hall with his Dad and turned toward Don and said, "Hi, Egghead!"

The astonished father looked to admonishing the boy for his crude behavior. Don intervened, got down on one knee in front of the boy, reminding him that, "Until you can take me downtown to Baskins and Robbins and buy me a milkshake, I am Mister Egg-head to you."

Don, father and son had a good chuckle over the matter, and a great lesson was learned; there is fun and games, but there is also respect. As Dad and son turned to walk away, the boy turned back toward Don and said, "I will, too, Mr. Egghead!"

Nobody will ever know for sure but positive relationships often steady the ship when push comes to shove dealing with students in negative situations. They provide a much better opportunity to deal with children on a one-on-one basis. It serves up the need for them to learn the accompanying requirement for respect.

Two years down the road, Don felt assured that Howard's efficient instructional programs created by the staff and led by the grade level leadership team, accomplished what he foresaw as being a highly successful elementary school. The staff had started a "back-to-back" instructional reading program with PE, music and counseling aiding in its development. Don sincerely thought that it was the envy of many elementary schools. Those connected with Howard were impressed with the direction the school was taking.

For those who might not know Don Essig too well, he does enjoy playing practical jokes. He even made merry with his two completely innocent American Eskimo miniature dogs (small size Huskies) that he and Janet had. These pranks often involved the "chippies" or chipmunks that frolicked about their yard. Don would point out the window and say, "There go some chippies!" Away the dogs would fly throughout the backyard looking for those evasive, deceiving little rodents, enjoying the chase as well as the confusion. Don was having as much enjoyment just watching their play and their antics as he had with a school's students in a similar fun-and-games situation.

Another go around for Don may have backfired when he teamed up with teacher Alan Conkey and they concocted what they thought would be a great comic caper on first grade teacher

Laurie Guttormsen and, unfortunately, her first graders.

It was Halloween and the two jokesters came up with a plan to go up into the attic of this first grade classroom while the first graders were outdoors for recess. When the kids had returned to class and were situated behind their desks a great hullabaloo erupted above them. A loud rumble of any manner of scary halloween noises came cascading down from the ceiling. The principal and his teacher cohort were having a heyday concocting eerie noises and laughter, ala "Friday the Thirteenth on Elm Street," or a scene from "The Exorcist"!

The ensuing picture below could not have been imagined by the two interlopers, and it wasn't part of the act! When they opened the ceiling hatch and looked down into the room they saw some highly frightened kids; some crying, some hiding under their desks, some not knowing what to do.

As bad as it was, the worst was yet to come, and it came in the form of a very angry first grade teacher who was not humored in any way by the prank. This practical joke climaxed when some scared students didn't even want to put on their costumes to walk around the school in the better organized "Halloween Parade."

It goes without saying, Don didn't think it was any fun either. He apologized profusely to the class and its teacher. He also spent the remainder of the afternoon calling all the parents of Laurie's kids to explain what took place, and to apologize to them for the ill-advised incident. He wanted the parents to know about the horseplay from the mouth of the horse before it came home in the children's version which might have called for a little revision.

Although this might have put a damper on further unthought out trickery by the principal and teachers, it didn't really put an end to any fun-for-all hijinks involving students and staff. The principal now proclaimed no more scary tricks on any more kids.

Despite all the trickery, the school was running smoothly. However, there are always those surprises that sometimes pop up. For starters, Don was notified by favorite counselor Jan Skuce that she had decided to go back to school full time. This meant that he was going to lose a very competent colleague. Next came the loss of a

PE teacher who wanted to move on to the high school to teach. Add that two grade-level team teachers were leaving the fold to go into international school teaching.

This left Don and the school with some important positions to fill. The personnel department came through with some big-time replacements, not only in the classroom, but a special fit with Carol Greig, a new sports and fitness specialist, to run the PE department. According to Don, she arrived at Howard with a bundle of new and different ideas on how to run the physical activities area.

The biggest concern for Don at this time was the problem he was having trying to find a replacement for Janet in the counselor's office. He was being very specific with the personnel office to get someone who, in his mind, could continue what he thought was a great program that Jan had created and developed.

One person stood out in his appraisal of all the candidates for the counseling position, but he was just completing graduate school. The personnel director said he felt that Stan Hultgren would probably want to return to the school where he formerly worked before attending grad school. Don studied Stan's resume and background and was convinced that Stan was the ideal one for the Howard counseling position.

There was a fly in the ointment. Stan had been made aware of the Howard opening, but he told personnel he wasn't sure he wanted to fill that counselor's slot. He just didn't seem very interested. So along comes Don on his positive thinking white horse. He telephoned Stan and asked if he would like to go pop-a-top at a local pub and they could talk about the job.

They met on a Saturday and had a great time sipping and talking at the "Good Times" tavern in Eugene. The times were so good that the good times have kept rolling ever since. Ask either of them now what they had talked about, and the best answer one can get is how good the "brewskies" were and how many they had downed!

What about the job? After the fermented hops had taken their toll on the tippler, Stan called personnel and said he wanted to go to Howard.

Thus began a long-standing Stan-Don friendship that exists to this day!

Yes, there were changes in 1974; staff moving on to other challenges and some teachers deciding to change grade levels. Through all this Don still felt positive that the overall competence and effectiveness of his staff had not changed one iota. Learning was strong and activities, including talent shows, had become big productions and fun for students and for faculty as well.

During this time Don worked with the regional director, Roy Rutter, in developing training activities and retreats for the nine principals of the regional schools: elementary, middle and the high school. This was an outcropping of his skills and practices acquired in the organization development doctoral program. He also continued to be a part of the district's communication cadre. On numerous occasions he was invited to speak statewide and share some of these ideas that he had formulated.

These speaking engagements became a catalyst as well as a background for a future full-time human relations consulting career.

This was a busy time for Don in professional involvement dealing with and about education in the state: he continued to announce athletic games for the University of Oregon Ducks. Not coming as a surprise, he and Janet kept a busy social calendar—ask anyone who might try to call in for a dinner date or a movie!

"Hey, great idea! Let me check my calendar and I'll get back to you. Go Ducks!" This was the usual rejoinder for such a quickie call or offer.

The Essig boys were getting older and maybe even a bit more demanding. They also were required to attend more school activities which might include sports. Janet was teaching at Spring Creek Elementary School in Eugene, and she too was having to attend all of her school functions.

It seems as though a busy person will always have some busy-body that wants to make them even busier. This time it was the newly hired Stan Hultgren that made a get busy offer that Don would be hard pressed to refuse. Stan's university advisor, Jerry Kranzler, had, so he said, "ocean view" property that was up in the

Cascade mountains. He wanted sell it.

While it really wasn't ocean view, it was located near Detroit Lake on Forest Service Land in the forested terrain. Jerry offered the property to Stan at a relatively low price. He explained that his family was getting older and not really interested in this mountain real estate any longer.

Stan approached Don to see if he and Janet might be interested in jointly buying into this mountain retreat with him. Stan couldn't afford to purchase the land on his own and offered to take Don to the mountain to check it out. Again, over a couple of brewskies, they could talk it over and see if they might be able to work out something together.

The cabin at Detroit Lake was situated in the forest along with some 60 other cabins. It was a very simple two story structure in some disrepair.

Jerry had it built but never did much improvement on the shell. There was no running water inside. No back deck, which made it about an eight foot drop from the back door to the ground. Upstairs insulation was still showing, and since there were no electrical connections, sun through the windows or a candle lit the indoors. In front was a piece of plywood that served as steps to the deck.

What they saw was a cabin shell that would need some elbow grease and sweat to make it into a livable, usable place to cabin-camp out.

On the way back home they concurred that it was in pretty good shape for the horrible shape it was actually in. They agreed it might provide a bundle of family enjoyment for vacation time. The extra work involved would create a lakeside mountain home to go to for casual rest and rehabilitation. Their conclusion was, "Yes! Let's do it."

Don, Janet and Stan became partners in a joint venture. This was far removed from Don and Stan working together at Howard. It is a partnership still ongoing. They put in a bundle of joint effort to bring their cabin dream into fruition. The cabin now has inside electricity and indoor plumbing, and is chock full of decorative items and trinkets that have been added by both families.

Don became known as the man who brought an extra wardrobe to school, each day! Why so, was the most egregious question? Don's answer included the disclaimer of not attempting to duplicate the oft-told story concerning actor John Wayne, although it came close.

Don frequented the halls of Howard, as he often did as he monitored the classrooms and tried to keep abreast of happenings in the school. He was in the first grade wing when he felt a need to answer the call of nature.

He stepped into the boys' restroom and was going about doing his business. In the next stall, a young lad was performing his act at the urinal, at first not noticing the school principal. When he saw Don he turned, still taking care of his nee, "Hi, Mr. Essig!"

Damage done. Don's pant leg and shoe was flushed in the excretion.

He had been whizzed on! The Duke would have been proud. Suffice it to say that from this point on Don always brought an appropriate change of clothing, just in case of a similar accident.

Don says he often regrets not getting that boy's name so that sometime in the future when that young man graduated from high school he could remind him of a time, 12 years earlier, when he had peed on the principal's leg!

Six years at Howard was a positive for Don in many ways. The skills he had learned in his doctoral program came up Aces! It included a wide variety of professionals he worked with and for, and he amassed a wide background of abilities that stood him in good stead for the ongoing steps in his professional life. As usual for Don, the next step came quicker than he thought it would, or quicker than he even imagined.

In early spring of 1978, North Eugene High School was going through a bit of staff turmoil. This was a school of fairly conservative values and traditions. The new three-year principal wanted to make a number of changes in the organization and systems of the school. Not everyone involved with the school, staff as well as some parents in the community, were up to accepting these alterations. The situation made for some uncomfortable relationships for all of those involved.

Really not according to protocol, but Tom Payzant, District Superintendent, invited himself to Don's house for lunch. It was even planned to occur at the kitchen counter, in Don's home! Talk about bumptiousness. But there was some acumen behind the behavior. Tom wanted the discussion that they were going to have to be private as possible.

The upshot was that Don was asked if he would be willing to take over the post as principal of North Eugene High School. Don admitted to only having elementary school experience, and he was concerned with how this move would fit in with the North Eugene staff.

Tom reiterated that he was not concerned about that aspect of Don's background. He said he needed someone that could bring the organization development skills to the North Eugene school.

"Think about it. Talk to some of your closest friends and to your family and then get back to me."

Don did, and readily got back to Tom with the conclusions he had received from all those he confided with, including those from his job exploratory list: "Take the job!"

Okay, now he had to cope with how all those skills he had learned and see if they would work with a staff four times the size of Howard! He also had to wrestle with the thought that the teachers and students he would primarily be dealing with had different educational backgrounds.

With a bit of fear and yet a great deal of confidence in his own abilities, Don took off on an undertaking with brand new challenges. It was a new professional beginning for Don Essig that began in 1978.

We temporarily interrupt this marriage to bring you "Fiddler on the Roof" April-May 1983

Right: Don (center stage clapping) as Papa in Fiddler on the Roof

Below: Second Birchwood home, 1978 and North Eugene graduation speech

CHAPTER EIGHT

North Eugene High School

"Show me a job without any pressure,
and I'll show you a job that's not a good job."

—John Wooden
UCLA Basketball Coach

Superintendent Payzant had a couple of somewhat surprising announcements to pass onto the Eugene community involving the school district. First, he was transferring elementary principal Don Essig to the head job at North Eugene High School. He followed this with the information that he also was moving each of the primary assistant principals in the four district secondary schools to a different high school. The result of this unexpected shuffle would move the number one assistant at South Eugene High School, Bill Personen, to joining up with Don at North Eugene.

The two really never knew each other beyond saying "hello" at district administrative meetings. When they met with Superintendent Payzant and Bill became aware of the change, his response to his new assignment not only impressed Don, it pleased him: "I've always been a company man," and that he would do whatever was necessary for him to fulfill his responsibility at the new school. This made it known to Don that he would have the support of at least one assistant in this school realignment.

"You did what? Left the nice, soft job as an elementary principal to move to the crazy pressures of the high school principalship!" According to Don these were the comforting words of a close friend when he found out that Don was not only switching roles, but he was leapfrogging over junior high school directly into the high school.

Not on very many occasions can one be found making the jump from the little kids to the biggest kids. Again, Don wrote about this transition for the 1983 issue of The Oregon Elementary Principal; "Sorry Teddy, There Is No Four-Square at the High School."

The next move for Don was to meet with the other two assistant principals, Betty Bergman and Dan Barnum. This group of North Eugene administrators agreed to meet together every other week for breakfast for the rest of the spring and early summer. They wanted to discuss what the future at North was going to be and to make plans to put into effect possible improvements that would involve students and staff.

They checked out each others' strengths and how they would fit into Don's administrative team idea. One change agreed upon was that they all would share in the student discipline problems. No one administrator would have all the negative duty. While being met with some trepidation, it later proved out to be a positive endeavor. Don was to take a share of the disciplinary duty which prompted the others to also take their fair share of the unpopular assignment.

The two holdover administrative assistants, Betty and Dan, were most helpful educating the newcomers on the traditions, programs and staff makeup, as well as describing the North Eugene community. The proposed morning sessions would prepare the newcomers for the transition and changes that were going to be made for the staff, come fall.

Don benefitted greatly from using his organization development strategy in assigning administrative tasks. Because of his limited experience at the secondary level, as principal he had to rely on the expertise of these assistants to carry out an administrative approach for the staff. Bill was to be the leader of the team in class scheduling. Betty would continue to be the matron to the community as well as to the various student groups within the school, and Dan would handle the school's finances.

Don's major strength was in planning the school budget and carrying out the overall financial planning and staff operations. He, obviously, was in charge of the overall organization of the administrative team. His role in carrying out communications with the staff and the community was a given. His wandering around style in the school should be a positive with the student body and there probably wouldn't be any more peeing on the pant leg incidents. But only because high school boys were a lot taller.

All the arrangements of duties would be publicized to the staff in the fall, and they all would be expected to meet with their respective administrator about any specific assignments they might have.

Any follower or compadre of Don Essig knows that he lives and thrives in an aura of positiveness. This again came to the fore with his assignment to North Eugene. Students from Howard Elementary first went to Kelly or to Madison Middle Schools; from there they were fed into North Eugene High School. This meant that after six years at Howard he would inherit some 250 former students who would be with him in the North Eugene student body. This would provide him with a modus operandi for taking the lead using his leadership style and his popular sense of humor. Of course, these kids told their friends who they were getting as a principal, and an appreciation of Don's unique personae could snowball.

Because of previous involvement in teaching organizations, and also including the activities and comradery with fellow members of his Congregational Church, Don was not moving into a completely strange staff environment. These positive connections worked in his favor in this his rookie year as a high school principal.

The department chairs at North met for two weeks before the opening of the school year. First, Don obtained Superintendent Payzant's permission to have an evening of dinner and planning at one of the city's restaurants. The purpose was to rename the group and, in turn, make it a "Staff Leadership Team." The acceptance of Don's signature program by these chairs would be a positive kickoff to his emergence as North's new head. This group had the most influence for possible changes or improvements to be made at the school.

Don offered his organization technique of putting on a wall butcher paper, then having everyone write their ideas about what was working well at North and what needed to be improved. These wall hangings could provide a great base for planning the entire school year. The whole process would be a positive from beginning to end. As Don so aptly pointed out, "it was a strategy not often used in other organizations."

All in all, the top four administrators at North agreed that these meetings were a positive approach to start off the school year. It helped immensely getting department heads on board with the new process.

This first year at the different school began smoothly, principally because Bill Personen did his new job at scheduling kids into their classes with alacrity. Don and Dan's operating budget and procedures were well in place and Betty Bergman had her student groups ready to meet and get started for the new year. The new principal gave a speech to the staff that seemed to be well accepted and later presented to the student body his list of expectations for them. All systems were on go and with that in mind, let the fun begin.

As the first week of school ended a long time tradition at North Eugene was about to begin. The opening week pep assembly featured the initiation of sophomore students into the school. A number of these neophytes, as selected through some constant unknown upperclassmen agenda, were to go out onto the gymnasium floor and push filberts across the floor, with their noses! While they were occupied with this endeavor, some students, probably seniors, continually pelted the pushers with handfuls of more filberts.

Why and how did such a hazing tradition get its start here at North?

Some say this practice was a tad easier, and somewhat more entertaining than being paddled, or dunked or being degraded in some other such manner.

Don gives the answer. The property where the school is located was on a filbert orchard north of Eugene. After construction, a few filbert trees were allowed to remain standing on the grounds. These trees offered fallen filberts for the students to pick up and throw at each other. Knowing the sometimes devious thinking of young juveniles, up popped the idea of a North Eugene Highlander hazing ceremony. From the trees came their initiation ammunition.

Part of the fun and games had to include, as can be expected, the new rookie principal taking his turn on the floor. Don said he was continuously bombarded with filberts. At the end of this fray he did come up with a few bumps and bruises and sores from the experience. He said it was all worthwhile because it allowed him to pick up some valuable, positive points with the North Eugene students.

Through this participation, Don also found out that it really was a fairly hazardous activity with potential physical dangers. He felt that maybe the school had been lucky that nobody had complained enough to prompt a lawsuit against the North Eugene school for endangering their children in this raucous action.

The following summer the filbert trees were removed because somehow the trees had become "diseased" and had to be cut down. Perhaps the powers-to-be also felt that this "disease" was contagious! Just maybe those trees could also cause some bumps and sores and bruises. Yeah, the trees as well as this North Eugene High School Highlander hazing tradition had to go.

His first year at North was successful and satisfying for Don. Some of his department leaders were using his organization development techniques in their own individual work. As a communication tool Don had started and wanted to continue the practice of having his "Monday Mumblings" dispersed to staff of weekly memos and happenings within the school and within the staff. These Mumblings were proven successful at Howard in keeping people informed and aware of "what was going on."

Don's sense of humor got the best of him, as it often does, and he manifested it one week when he decided to write the "Mumblings" all in phonetics; every word misspelled but with the word sound being correct when read aloud. Some thought it funny. Others, mainly in the English Department, were a bit appalled at this intentional dispersion of the English language. They complained, gently, of course, to the principal that they saw little humor in this little ruse. They say that time heals all wounds, and in a very short time the English staffers picked up on the fun and began sending phonetically prepared messages to Don!

The "Mumblings" sometimes played the clown with repartee or cartoons that applied to some part or aspect of the school. The flow of this tomfoolery picked up with the staff and they began to take another look at life, finding new and different ways to enjoy working at North Eugene. All this went on before the emergence of personal computers. The principal's drollery had its Monday mumblings typed out on Don's Olympic typewriter with copies distributed to the staff in their school mail boxes. On some occasions the material would be hand distributed so that Don could get the chance to see some of the staff personally. In this computer age, one has to wonder if schools still have individual mailboxes for their staffs.

One of the personal situations that Don picked up on throughout the school year was the major difference in the use of time compared to the elementary school. He found out that it probably was because of the size differential. It took considerably more time working with 100 staff members instead of 25, dealing with 1,000 students compared with 400, and communicating with the total North Eugene community instead of just Howard School families. Don could also throw in the three-to-five nights a week with school activities as opposed to one-night-a- month PTA meetings at the elementary school. Put these all together and it can become a big change in personal time logistics problems.

With all things considered, it was a very satisfying year for Don Essig. He had fewer discipline problems than he imagined he would have had. Most of the staff bought into his OD strategies, and he felt that he had a great administrative team.

However, into each life, even a positive one, a little rain has to fall. One of the very few negatives which stood out that school year was the Highlander football team wiich won only one game all season! Most of the parents were willing to accept the fact that North Eugene players were very young and had little or no experience. OK, that sounds reasonable, especially since the very next year they won the league title!

In the spring of Don's first year at North, he had an unexpected visitor from the University of Oregon's School of Education. Barbara Wilcox was from the special education department that worked directly with the parents of children with severe physical handicaps. She had a program that the administration had accepted to have Don and his school initiate a class for bringing severely handicapped students onto the high school campus. Superintendent Payzant had convinced Barbara that the North Eugene school was the best place to put the new program because of its very accepting staff and innovative administrative personnel to make it work.

Don found out early on that he didn't have any preliminary say in the setting up of the program. With that in mind, he and his people went straight to the task of planning strategies for bringing to the rest of the staff and the student body the plans for incorporating the new students into the school. There would be thirteen students brought into the school activities, food and transportation services, and even into a few of the regular classes.

Don felt strongly that it was most important that everyone at the school become savvy of what was transpiring so that these new students would not be looked upon as a disruption to their school and cause some unnecessary interactions within the school.

Another hot-water-brainstorm for Don came while warming

up his soul and body in Assistant Principal Dan Barnum's backyard hot tub. In fact, it was Dan that offered the suggestion that Don grabbed on to: "Make this an opportunity and not a burden" should be the theme, and that was the message Don took to the staff, students and community. It was also a slogan Don continued to use when he later went into his own consulting business. This phrase was also used as a title for an article he submitted to Educational Leadership.

Don started off by telling his audience that there was a lot to be learned from having handicapped students on campus. It provided a chance for everyone to learn more about severely handicapped people, and how best they can become part of where they live and work and go to school. The communication process took hold. He convinced his people that it was all about making life an opportunity and not a burden.

John McDonald became the special education teacher. Most of the educational activities took place in his classroom. This special program opened up the opportunity for some of the regular students to sign up and serve as tutors for John's classes. He was the catalyst for communicating his program and bringing it to the entire student body. According to Don, the tutors who were selected to assist John were exceptional in sharing with other students exactly what was happening in this unique class.

At the first student pep assembly of this school year Don prepared a speech in which he gave a brief explanation of the special needs class. He then had each of the handicapped students be introduced to the student body.

They were escorted, one at a time, to the front of the gymnasium and then were introduced by a popular student; football player, rally squad member, drama student, or student body officer. By the end of the third introduction the entire gymnasium was standing, applauding and cheering each presentation. For the next five years, according to Don, he only had one disciplinary problem between a regular student and a special needs student.

Don had the bragging rights; it was proven beyond a doubt that North Eugene was a great school to test out the new strategies of having severely handicapped students in the entire school program. An important aspect of this special union was that he insisted that, although most of these students were housed in elementary schools, the parents were encouraged to send their teenagers to school looking like high school students. They cooperated with the idea and, in most cases, it was difficult to distinguish the special kids from the regular students.

Many high schools in Oregon took up the idea and plan of North Eugene and started similar "handicap" classes. Schools shared the same techniques with school administrators and staffs to make it work. Eventually, what Barbara and her staff produced expanded into other states.

In 1981, Don was awarded the Oregon Special Education Principal of the Year award presented by Barbara Wilcox's staff at their convention. As Don has frequently pointed out, it was an award deserved and should be shared with the total North Eugene High School staff and student body, as well as with the North Eugene community.

Don's second year at North Eugene started off with a lot more consternation than anyone had ever expected. A completely new and disparate challenge that upset the living equilibrium of many people in the city of Eugene, and not just the teaching element, came to town. This internecine event came down on Don and his administrative staff and faculty, the same as it did at other schools in the district, and did not put Don or the Eugene school district in a very positive position.

The organized teachers in Eugene went on strike against the school district!

Two weeks of school planning with department heads and a week with the staff, which included a humorous skit put on by the administration on the last day of school planning, precluded any knowledge Don and his staff might have had involving the immediate days ahead. No one knew, nor had a clue what the future held, or if their lives might significantly change.

A meltdown of salary and benefits discussions between the Eugene school board's negotiation team and representatives for the Eugene teachers union began what was to become a two-week strike by the teachers' against the school district.

Maybe both sides should have taken a peek at what happened in nearby Corvallis the year before, 1978, when negotiators for the teachers and the school board settled their differences only 3 hours into the strike. Corvallis Schools' Superintendent Tom Wogaman decided that that half-day work stoppage by the teachers would constitute an in-service day, with nothing lost. Incidentally, that half-day sit-down went into the record books as the shortest strike in the state's history!

The Eugene strike gave a sinking feeling to Don. Starting the 1979-1980 school year, he was going into the school building with some of his staff members parading out front with picket signs and negative chanting that tied into the strike. It also hurt because Don and his administrative team had a much different impression of the school teaching staff so soon after concluding some very positive planning sessions the previous week.

This wasn't going to be easy for the districts' administrators as well as for the teachers. It definitely wasn't a positive that classroom plans and student agendas were being put on hold. However, what the teachers gained from this strike venture would also, indirectly, flow down to the school district's administrative employees. The teachers and administrators were hired and rewarded by the services they were hired to fulfill. They each had their individual responsibilities to carry out, in good times and bad; strike or no strike, Corvallis or Eugene.

This was going to be a tough ride, for as Tom Wogaman pointed out, he had substitutes on hold to use in the perceived absence of his teachers if the Corvallis strike persisted. He hoped he would not have to use them because of the animosity and negativity that would envelope the Corvallis schools. He lucked out; the Eugene schools didn't.

As Don so aptly put it, the two-week schools' shutdown was much more difficult than anyone could have realized. He had some staff picketing outside his school and chanting comments about the unsuccessful negotiations. He also had to attend daily briefings for all district administrators. To compound the already existing difficulties and its implications, the school board decided the schools would be reopened the next week with substitute teachers taking over the district's classrooms.

This was a challenging time for all the employees and positive Don and his employee entourage were no exception. He and his team had to use defensive tactics at the doors of the school to forestall confrontations between staff teachers and the substitutes as they arrived in the parking lot and were debarking from the buses. Added to this mixture of animosity was that a large number of students arrived at the school, took sides with the striking teachers, and refused to enter the building or attend classes.

During this hectic time he had to maintain composure with his staff, attend numerous and sundry school board meetings, deal with daily upheavals and changes with substitutes, and pray and prepare for the eventual return to normalcy for his school after the strike.

From the very beginning, Don tried to maximize the thinking that if a strike should occur, it was not and would never be an uprising between administrators and staff. To his way of thinking, it was a conflict between the citizen-selected school district Board of Directors and the teacher-selected negotiators for the Eugene teachers' union.

Don's comments to his staff before the strike made the transition back to work after the walkout much easier than what was reported as happening at other schools. On the first day back for contracted teachers Don made it perfectly clear at a full staff meeting that the important work of teaching and learning was again going to be the first priority. He emphasized that any negative behaviors exhibited during the strike was history and would not, in any way, continue to exist. All relationships between North Eugene educators; administrators, teachers and/or staff would be on a positive note and in a positive manner. These pre-strike and post-strike remarks by North Eugene's principal brought out a more reasonable and positive relationship between all the school's groups for the remainder of the school year.

As a sign of helping to bring the school back to normalcy after the walkout, Don sent out an edict to the staff that everyone wear some sort of costume for the upcoming Halloween days. This request seemed to be a relatively normal requisite for Don to send out. After all, he oversaw the wearing of such regalia along with the students ever since the beginning of his elementary school days. Some of the North Eugene staff, with their noses in the air, didn't buy into the program: What kind of horse puckey was this, acting up along side the students?

When the big masquerade day arrived, Don came into the school about 6:45 in the morning wearing his Halloween costume. He was surprised to find the parking lot full of cars. Entering the building, no one could be seen, anywhere! Going into his office he was greeted by a staffer who admonished him for being late to the Halloween party now in progress in the auditorium!

Going into the auditorium with the lone staff member, Don almost fell into shock. The immediate rows of the facility were loaded with his entire staff, and they were all wearing the exact masks: Don's face!! Someone had obviously obtained a mug-shot of Don, had it blown up and made copies to face-size which, in turn, made life-size masks for the staff. The shock and surprise brought resounding laughter that could be heard throughout the school. They had bought into his program of Halloween attire, and again this added to the positive relationship he maintained with the staff throughout the remainder of the school year.

Some can come up with stunning and invigorating ideas when just soaking in the bathtub or in the shower. Don says he sometimes does his best thinking in these type of situations. For instance, while in a warm shower he thought out a plan for helping needy families in the North Eugene area: a North Eugene High School "Project Give" that would take place during the Christmas holiday season. It would involve competition between classes to see who could accumulate the most canned food and the most money to help those who might be in need of some special assistance.

The local Safeway store chipped in by helping to provide a reduced priced turkey for each of the needy families identified. This generosity also included boxes of canned food items.

Another North staff member quite possibly took the same type of hot water idea-refresher coming up with a plan of having each teacher in the school decorate their classroom door with a motivational decor to publicize and promote the giving project.

The hot baths ideas combined to make this grand plan of food gift-giving a huge success! There were some 50 families that benefited from this Christmastime largesse instigated by the high school. When Don returned to the school for the annual North Eugene High School December Retirees Social in 2011, he could see "Project Give" was still going strong, 32 years after its incubation in Don's hot water shower in 1979.

Despite the difficult beginning, the 1979-1980 school year ended on a highly positive note. The next year would open with no teacher contract negotiations and certainly with no teacher strike in mind. In fact, the next four years at North were filled with changes and much positive growth in the attitude of staff, students and parents, as well as with the community at large. Continuous positive communication made the total educational process work and stay up to date.

The biggest alteration for the district's schools was the inclusion of freshmen into the high school starting with the 1983-84 school year. This was a result of the school district reorganizing their kindergarden through twelfth grade alignment which involved integrating the freshmen from the middle schools. This came as a huge change for the North Eugene staff.

With all the planning by each department, the administrative and leadership teams, the inclusion of the freshmen began with very few glitches. It now provided a chance for the administrative team to add a number of female teachers to departments that didn't have any. The ongoing positive commitment that had already been established made the major change a big success.

To date, all the Eugene high schools still include the four-year curriculum in their teaching agendas.

A final touch to Don Essig's six-year tenure at North Eugene was his participation with the students in the school's spring musical, "Fiddler on the Roof." Laurie Guttormsen, North's drama director, asked if he would perform in the school production as one of the "papas." He agreed to take on the part with the understanding he didn't have to attend all the rehearsals because of his principalship commitments. Laurie acquiesced. In response Don grew a beard, which came out sort of gray and scraggly. He also let his hair grow out long for the role.

His face appeared on advertisements for the production. He assisted in soliciting funds for the play as well as provide some needed funds for the drama department which was about eight thousand dollars in the red from previous presentations.

The school's "Fiddler on the Roof" was a box office smash! It sold out all six performances. The play received additional generous donations that shot the production and the department five thousand dollars into the black! The school now had a cushion to work with for future presentations.

North Eugene's administration established a new and welcomed relationship with the music and drama departments.

Don and Janet have attended all the 10 and 20-year reunions of his senior classes at North Eugene. Many have become good friends of the Essigs despite the age differences

Throughout the years of his principalships, Don was satisfied knowing that the organizational development concepts, ideas and activities he espoused actually worked. For six years at North Eugene High School he had an administrative team and a leadership group that believed in and worked on these goals, and it was most satisfying to him.

Don had moved and changed on a number of occasions in his education and teaching career from 1960 to 1984. In his sixth year at North Eugene he again got the Essig family traveling itch to move on to something different. With this in mind he accepted a position in the Eugene District Office as Director of Management Services with the appointing support of District Superintendent Margaret Nichols. In this new position he would be working directly with all of the district's administrators.

This appointment ended Don Essig's career as a high school administrator. He admitted at the conclusion of his high school principalship that it had been one of the most satisfying, and great opportunities of his professional life.

Right: Don giving presentation to school staff on budget reductions

Below: Education Center office (using favorite typewriter)

CHAPTER NINE

Moving to District Office

*"You have not done enough, you've never done enough,
so long as you have somthing more to contribute."*

—Dag Hammershold
UN Secretary General

Even changing jobs within the same school district can bring a mixed bag of emotions. Leaving one position that a person has been doing for twelve years, working directly with teachers and staff can become quite discombobulating. On the other hand, a different and unknown set of circumstances could prove to be most exhilarating for a progressive, positive thinking employee, like Don Essig.

Don's move to the district office's Education Center did not necessarily make him a first-timer in the building. The office he moved into was about 20 short steps from where he and friend Dick Arends worked halftime with the Differentiated Staffing project back in 1969 to 1972. The major locale difference for him in his new office was that he now had windows, plus the office was larger. It took awhile for Don to be informed of just what his new duties would entail. He did know he was to be in the human resources department and who his district supervisor would be.

When it finally came down, Don would spend some of his time working with building administrators on the organizational techniques he learned and practiced in the DS project. In addition, he was told he would be involved with the communications cadre that he and Arends had setup back in 1972. On the plus side of being involved with the leadership cabinet, he also would be able to keep in touch with district operations and in decision making.

In December of 1984 Don was designated as the district's contact person with the Oregon State Legislature during their capitol lawmaking sessions. He now was part of the Oregon School Board lobbying team working to improve educational benefits for Oregon school districts. This new assignment packed him off into a wide swath of directions and purposes.

Don became involved in a plethora of community, state, and other nonprofit functioning groups. He joined Rotary and got caught up in their activities and fundraising projects. As far as the district was concerned, he was on a roll to provide a positive image of the Eugene School District to the community and to answer questions raised involving the district's programs and goals.

His community participation, along with the continuing role of public address announcing for University of Oregon Duck athletics, put him into a position of accepting numerous speaking engagements for a variety of community groups, talking about public education, as well as Oregon athletics. He was in a speech making demand in the community world, as well as in the Webfoot world of college sports. Being the master of ceremonies at many engagements promulgated his positive and gregarious life style.

He was kept very busy in this new domain. He was now outside the daily stress of student discipline, building operations and direct teacher-parent confabs. Evening obligations were reduced significantly, and now many home activities included those that were involved with his own boys, Scott and Ted. He could very well have gone to some of Janet's meetings and parent conferences, just to keep his hands in, and to keep himself up to snuff!

New responsibilities always seemed to find a way to pop up. The district was heading into multiple budget cuts that was going to involve a number of school staffs. His new situation was to put together a presentation that would bring out his past training and background. In this new assignment he would use overhead color slides that would show school staffs the facts and figures enabling them to better understand the potential budget changes.

His presentation at North Eugene High School produced the same litany and expectations as was discussed at all the other high schools, except for a singular exception. The end of his program which was eagerly anticipated, brought out a "welcome home" surprise gathering in recognition of Don's six-year principalship at the school!

There was an abundance of food and drink. The party concluded with a tear-jerking gift from the staff to Don Essig: a large picture of him drawn by a staff member and signed by the entire staff. That picture remains as a tender reminder of those wonderful, positive years he had shared with the faculty, staff and the students at North Eugene.

In the summer of 1981, Don attended a conference in Claremont, California, that was sponsored by the Institute for Development of Educational Activities (I/D/E/A). There were some 200 administrators from throughout the United States in attendance. This gathering became a mainstay in Don's work and affiliation in this human relations arena which included an expansive national network of participating colleagues.

He continued attending these conferences for the next 13 years! A crowning feature of these many I/D/E/A sessions came when he and three other participants staged a musical and informational program for the 25th anniversary of I/D/E/A.

As Don would say, the I/D/E/A conferences were, hands down, the major catalyst leading to his success as a national and international speaker and consultant.

Don continued doing a wide range of activities in the Eugene district's education center. He also began accepting assignments from across Oregon to conduct lessons in differentiated staffing and organization development and how they might be incorporated into administrative practices.

Don was invited to speak at the 1986 I/D/E/A conference. The upshot of this successful presentation was that he decided that he soon wanted to go to half-time employment with the school district. By doing this it would allow him to move forward with his own planned consulting business and start marketing himself as a speaker on a much wider scope throughout the United States.

Above: Bumper sticker given to clients. Old lady/young lady picture "Perception is everything". I/D/E/A Fellows attendee, Claremont, CA, 1989

Above: I/D/E/A quartet, 1992, left to right, Bob Winters, Dean Welin, Don and Gayle Anderson

CHAPTER TEN

On the Road to a Consulting Business

"I don't know if a positive attitude works all the time,
but a negative one does."

—**Roger Crawford**
Motivational Speaker

Although Don spent a number of years as a school administrator after acquiring his PhD, it was also in 1971 that he saw the beginning of his consulting career. He continued working half-time for the Eugene school district and as a research assistant for the Center for Advanced Study of Educational Administration at the University. He, along with other members of CASEA, were often requested to give presentations throughout the country concerning Oregon's burgeoning staffing and organization project. This was when Don started formulating programs that included the use of projector slides and a variety of informational handouts.

In the Beaverton, Oregon, school district, Don, along with his good friend and member of the District's communication cadre, Jack Pynes, did a program for an elementary school staff on communication, problem solving and decision making. In a manner of speaking the presentation "brought the house down," according to Lee Christiansen, Assistant Superintendent in Beaverton, who had arranged the seminar. He and Don had been doctoral students together at the University of Oregon.

Don and Jack's presentation style included humor and the earthy experiences that they had had with Eugene elementary school staffs. It was a top drawer performance that helped persuade Don into becoming a full-time speaker and human relations consultant. It didn't happen right away but a spark was set off to eventually move his positive lifestyle into that direction.

Throughout his career as an administrator he was invited to speak at many conferences throughout Oregon. At the Oregon Wellness Conference in Seaside, put on by the Oregon State Department of Education, Don's workshop, "Make Life an Opportunity, Not a Burden," became one of the most popular and well attended sessions during the week.

He built his offering around many of the ideas promulgated by the staffing and organization project in Eugene. He expanded his talk with differing educational cartoons directed toward the majority of teachers who were in attendance. Music-related tapes were added along with many of his personal experiences as a teacher and administrator.

Don continued his appearances at the workshop for the next seventeen years, becoming almost a fixture at the Seaside wellness gathering. He also was invited to be the keynote speaker at some of the sessions.

As a result of this conference, he was selected to give talks at a number of school districts in Oregon and Washington. For this, Don says he is grateful to Len Tritsch and Jo Wilson of Oregon's Department of Education for their encouragement and their influence and support in pushing him onward in his quest to become a full-time public speaker.

The education department began another wellness conference, this time for senior citizens. The attendees came from senior centers located throughout the Pacific Northwest. A few also attended from other nearby states in hopes of eventually starting up similar conferences in their own areas.

Don's amalgamation of stories, tunes and cartoon projections also became a must-see for the over-60 crowd. An offshoot of this incursion into senior town was that he garnered speaking and presiding invitations at a number of other senior conclaves throughout the United States.

Time can sometimes become a problem; either too much, or too little. For Don it was a case of too little. Everything he was doing and what he had to do didn't put a curb on his energy or vitality. There just wasn't enough time to give full, positive reinforcement to his many and sundry pursuits.

Being a full-time principal, a full-time husband and parent, a part-time public speaker as well as a sports public address announcer for Oregon football and basketball games found Don coming up short on carrying out all his commitments. He decided he had to turn down some speaking invites as well as other engagements. Don said that in all honesty he actually had to set aside some periods of time to be able to sit down and socialize and be with his and Janet's close friends.

As he continued attending workshops and wellness conferences, he continued to polish up his slides and music shows that he used in public presentations.

As had been noted earlier, Eugene principal Max Beninga told him about the educational activities conference in Claremont, California. Because Max couldn't attend he urged Don to go in his stead, all paid for by the district. This particular conference provided Don with the opportunity to hear and evaluate a variable potpourri of presentations. It was the springboard he needed in his thinking about a personal career as a public speaker.

Don became colleagues with many educators from around the country. Among these was Dean Welin from California. With Dean, it was a bit scary how similar they were in personal and professional attributes. This was attested to by the observations of their respective marriage partners. As a result of this meeting Don and Dean developed a close friendship that continues today.

Attending so many conferences, Don accumulated a multitude of ideas and suggestions that he filed away to be used in future presentations and speaking engagements. He judiciously evaluated and graded the many styles he saw and heard from other speakers.

The 1982 Claremont conference brought four new acquaintances into the Essig fold. One might wonder if, along the way, he brought out any long-term antagonists, or enemies into his lifetime arena. It might be difficult to produce such a nemesis when dealing with a person so wrapped up in such a shroud of positiveness. The new grouping of buddies made up a quartet that not only gave individual speeches, but also joined up to write song lyrics and then performing them about other speakers and their performances.

Teaming up with Don in forming this singing-speaking quartet was Dean Welin from California; Robert Winters of Michigan, and other various attendees. They performed their act for nine years at these conferences. The high water mark for this performing group, adding Gayle Anderson, came into fruition at the 1992 Claremont program that celebrated the 25th year of the Institute for the Development of Educational Activities Conference. These singing orators proved so popular that they continued doing their act at five other conference sites throughout the country. Another, Gib Stuve from Southern California, also became a significant member of Don's new group of friends.

Still another fellow troubadour, from Claremont, was George Iannacone of New Jersey. George brought Don to the Northeast part of the country on numerous speaking sojourns. His "Make Life an Opportunity" and "Lead, follow, or get out of the way" seminars became a rousing success wherever he went on education missions. It was just another kickoff to his becoming a speaker who could crisscross the country presenting his speaking wares.

The Don-Dean-Bob-Gib buddies became a partnership of four men with diverse backgrounds who moulded themselves into a foursome of caballeros brought together by very similar lives and interests. At this writing they have all celebrated at least 50 years with their original spouses, which is quite an accomplishment considering their traveling from place to place and all the individual plans and undertakings that they were involved in.

After ending their Claremont attendances the group came together to perform at one another's retirement gatherings, and even at other individual gigs over the years. Don's mountain cabin became a group rest and rehabilitation center for the balladeers, as well as at other places they chose, such as Lake Tahoe in Nevada, Essexville (no way tied in with Don and his family), as well as other sacred havens in Michigan. They secreted away in southern and northern California and at a hideaway in Banff, British Columbia. According to Don, this has all been a great go-around with a close knit group, and it provided many enduring memories that he said he would cherish.

In 1987 Don discussed the possibility with Superintendent Margaret Nichols about his staying on in the Eugene school district, but only on a halftime basis. He was on task to begin his personal speaking and consulting business into a serious, although halftime, endeavor.

She agreed to the arrangement, even offering a number of hints and suggestions on how he could make his consulting career a success. The Superintendent's contacts with other administrators in the state and throughout the country could help him immeasurably in starting up in a relatively new career.

Right: Don's book written for support staff members

Below: Motivational Minutes book by Successories, 1994

PERSONAL EXCELLENCE for KEY PEOPLE

by Don M. Essig, Ph.D.

SUCCESSORIES®
~148~
MOTIVATIONAL MINUTES
~WRITTEN BY DON ESSIG~
Insightful ideas for improving the quality of your life.

Above: Don on the speakingcircuit

Right: Consulting brochure designed by Amy Daniel Marketing, 1992

DON ESSIG

You should hear this guy talk!

CHAPTER ELEVEN

A Career in Consulting

*"Far and away, the best prize that life offers
is the chance to work hard at work worth doing."*

—Theodore Roosevelt
US President

Throughout Don's career as a teacher, principal and central office administrator, he was ever conscious of the importance of staff members at every place he was employed. Labeled "classified employees," they were the secretaries, food service, bus drivers, teacher aides and custodial members of the staff. He determined that these employees were going to be treated as equals in each of his staff acquirements. In his CASEA training programs he emphasized that these employees be included along with the teachers and administrators at each location of training,

Don relayed his feelings that although these persons' pay and benefits were often much less than the other professional staff, they were still a strong, productive element of every organization. He was adamant about classified employees being treated as professionals in the field of education.

Don parlayed his professional feelings and attitudes toward all types of employees he worked for and with, using another of his well-known mantras, "Make life an opportunity, not a burden." He often states that to him this statement stands for and leads into positive conceptions, communications and personal self-esteem.

The inclusion of these classified staff members in his training program prompted him to write a book dealing specifically with this type laborer. As a result of his writing and planning, Don was introduced to John Brown, the Director of the Oregon Classified Employees Association. In talks with Brown, he was encouraged to continue with his developmental ideas and present them to Brown for inclusion in a statewide training program available to members of the OSAA.

As a continuum, Don finished writing a training manual "Personal Excellence for Key People". His former colleague at Howard Elementary School, Dennis Arendt, provided the artwork which included caricatures of the former fellow employees as they might have appeared at work. This booklet, along with a number of offerings of his other program presentations, evolved into a three-hour program for classified employees, named after the title of his book.

Continuing to work with Brown and the OSAA, Don was booked into a number of school districts throughout Oregon, presenting his PEKP program exclusively for classified employees. The pioneer program resulted in his becoming a popular presenter of OSAA programs at regional and statewide conferences. These programs, so he was told, resulted in many attendees growing in self-esteem and positive feelings about themselves and their work in their chosen professions.

Don's efforts in writing and in presentations began to expand. Attendees at conferences from other states along with invitations from his I/D/E/A buddies had him giving presentations throughout the United States. He boasted that his favorite presentation was to the National Association of School Food Services Employees in Las Vegas, Nevada, where he received a standing ovation from nearly 1500 attendees.

Perhaps his most embarrassing moment on the speaking circuit was at his presentation to the Oregon School Secretaries' Association convention. His former secretary at Howard School, Edith Traynor, was the president of the state association and invited him to be the keynote speaker. Before introducing Don to the attendees, she asked Don to come to the stage and put a paper bag on his hand while she did the introduction. Don stood there for a few minutes while Edith expounded about her former boss. Then she closed her introduction with, "And I want all of you to know that until today, I've never been able to get Don in the sack." Don stood there with a red face and his mouth wide open, while the audience howled in laughter. He finally composed himself and amazingly was able to do the presentation. This was probably the best example of the great working relationship, filled with humor, that he and Edith had for his six years at Howard School.

Along with his classified employees, program he persisted with his repertoire at the Wellness Conferences in Seaside, and they were being seen and heard by wellness advocates from other states. Now he was being invited to other Wellness Conferences throughout the country. All this, plus his consulting work, was beginning to take off in a very positive direction with speaking engagements every month!

Hey, and don't forget to include his speaking engagements in Autzen Stadium and at MacArthur Court! Somewhere along the line Don Essig has to contribute to home and hearth, as well as with his friends outside his workaday world.

In June, 1990, Don officially retired from the Eugene School District and took on the more limiting career of being a full time presenter. His many experiences from a Doctoral program and through the CASEA team, his attendance at the I/D/E/A conferences, and his 30 years as a teacher and administrator built a strong base for his moving from teacher-presenter to being a consultant. Don maintains that throughout his consulting career he was able to use his skills as an educator to full benefit as a presenter. His postulation was: "A successful consultant is simply a successful teacher."

Don moved forward in this ambitious undertaking that had

started out as part time. At the recommendation of Stuart Lomski, a Eugene business owner, he was initiated into the Emerald Executive Association, a business leaders group, with members from differing professions in the Eugene area.

Through this affiliation he processed his speaking career into the business world. Over his 24 years of EEA membership, his speaking-counseling foray expanded. His role as the popular Oregon Duck athletic announcer made him even a more rounded and popular presenter, now working with a diversified array of professions rather than just with educators and senior citizens.

With his membership in EEA, Don wanted to expand his program to support staff employees in the private business world. These employees were often treated as second-class workers. He wanted to reverse this thinking and attitude of business owners and managers of companies in EEA by presenting his personal excellence program to their support staffs.

There was a small problem that confronted Don in this new plan. His PEKP was written exclusively for school employees and would be extremely difficult to implement for other business or professional groupings.

What's a fella to do? Embarking on a new project, he began rewriting and reprinting his personal excellence book in a more generic pattern, one that could be used with any group of support staff professionals, educationwise or otherwise.

Don turned to fellow Emerald Association member, Eugene Print Company owner Robert Morris. Together they created an attractive cover and, again, with the assistance of Arendt, they altered some of the books' picture caricatures. An improved "Personal Excellence for Key People" was reborn. Now Don began marketing and promoting his PEKP seminar package to the business world as well as to nonprofit organizations. It soon became a highly popular program.

Another "ah-ha" moment in Don's psychi took him in another direction. After consultations with some EEA members, he began exploring the possibility of developing a program in leadership advancement. With ideas from his "Make Life an Opportunity" sessions, and from notes he had taken from I/D/E/A gatherings, his leadership agenda began to take shape.

His program got off the dime and began to move forward when he was invited to give his presentation to some of the EEA member managers and supervisors within their own companies.

Don incorporated a number of summaries and anecdotes from personal events related to his past experiences and practices as a principal in the schools he served. Using these stories and other tales from school made his program more meaningful for all the participants. His communication problem solving, as well as decision-making instruments and techniques had participants going back to their jobs well fortified with new skills and ideas. He was able to get across his idea "There is no good leader who is not a good teacher." This concept was a direct connection to his own personal background.

So, where to now? With another consultant and former educator, Paul Plath, a new consulting scheme was created and developed: a Chamber of Commerce Leadership Program. This came about after having been contacted by the Eugene and the Springfield Chambers of Commerce. They were asked to present eight full-day sessions, one each month from September to June for some 30 participants from the Eugene-Springfield metropolitan areas. Don continued in this program for five continuous years into the early 2000s.

This experience paid huge dividends, as it allowed him to work with a large number of future leaders of the community. He was able to observe their personal growth as they moved forward into management positions.

Don is a people person. If asked what he had taken away and what he had learned from his consulting practices he'll undoubtedly say, "people are much the same irrespective of their working arrangements. The same problems and successes exist in all professions because that is where human beings are located and are functioning."

He added that it doesn't make a bit of difference what they do on the job. "People have to communicate, solve problems, make decisions, try to get along with each other, and try to make the workplace a location where one can go everyday and enjoy every minute they are there."

The rewards lining the walls and book shelves in the Essig home attest to their being influential members of many clubs and activities. Don was president of the Oregon Club in 1989, dedicated to raising money for the University's athletics. It was about this time that he was a member of the Board of Directors for the Oregon State University Alumni Association. He also served on the Board of Directors for the University of Oregon Alumni Association. Janet is a longtime member of the "Daisy Ducks," a university booster club that supports Oregon athletics by providing scholastic scholarships. They both are very active members of the First Congregational Church and Eugene Country Club serving on a variety of committees and Boards.

Don confided to Heather Roberts, a student in Journalism at UO who was writing an article about Don as a class assignment, that, out of a "current total of 1,310 events over the past 45 years, he has announced nearly every single Oregon men's football and basketball game." Needless to say, she was surprised he had done that many Oregon athletic events.

Don currently spends his extracurricular time, outside his professional endeavors, golfing, reading and being engaged in motivational public speaking. He had a "Motivational Minutes" segment on KPNW-AM, a radio station out of Eugene. He recorded 543 different Minutes, beginning in 1994 until March 9, 2012, when sponsorship was cancelled because of budget cuts. His 148 Motivational Minutes book was published in 1994 by Successories in Chicago.

Above: The Lone Deranger, Ken Hoiland

Above middle: Don & Jerry Allen, Duck radio announcer

Above right: Don & John Dick, 1939 All-American Duck basketball player

Right: Don in the Pit, last week before closing

Far right: Groundbreaking for Matthew Knight Arena, left to right, Pat Killkenny, Don, Phil Knight and Dave Frohnmayer

CHAPTER TWELVE

Scenes from McArthur Court

*"Without any doubt this is the finest barn
I've ever worked in."*

—Bob Hope
Famous Comedian

The first unofficial and opening scene for Don behind the mike in old McArthur Court was, in its own way, quite auspicious. On the night of December 1, 1967, he was the first of three male contestants vying for the job as the Oregon Duck's Public Address Announcer. This beginning foray into announcing for UO was an Oregon loss to New Mexico University, 64-60.

Athletic Director Norv Ritchey tried for better luck with the other two potential PA announcers in the next two games. Results from those two game encounters aren't remembered, only that the winning candidate for the PA job was announced the following Monday, December 10, when Norv called Don and told him "You're going to be our guy!" Thus began the saga of Don Essig, official University of Oregon Athletic Public Address Announcer for the next 45 years and counting.

Mac Court back in those days was a much different venue than it was when it finally closed its doors making way for the spanking new Matthew Knight Arena in 2010. The lighting in "Old Mac" was poor but it didn't matter because few, if any, games were televised from the Duck home court.

Don's announcing position in the old arena was at the press table on the second level, behind the student section. He frequently pointed out that he "had the best seat in the house" for watching the game.

Don remembered that the Ducks weren't very good in his first year, finishing with a 7-19 season. This didn't diminish his excitement for working the games after so many previous years in Mac Court as a spectator. He had always hoped to someday announce the games himself.

The year 1967 brought in one of Oregon's greatest recruiting classes. Coming on board were such stars as Stan Love, Bill Drozdiak, Larry Holliday and a host of others. The Duck world was abuzz with great expectation for the basketball future. In those days the incoming freshmen played separately from the varsity until their sophomore year. What was really odd back then, according to Don's recollection, was that the freshmen game drew in some 8,000 fans with only about 3,000 remaining for the varsity encounter.

The years 1968-69 brought in some big changes to Mac Court. It became nosier, the student section became rowdier and the band became bigger and louder--all this coming from the perspective of the public address announcer. However, the place was sold out for nearly every game!

There was much more for the Webfoot fans to cheer about with their team going 13-13, a lot better than the previous losing seasons. A negative aspect of this new excitement for the public address and press side reporters was that the students were becoming more involved and standing for the entire game. This was great for the team but entailed Don and the press corps to have to stand to view and report on the floor action. Don was continually asked by an administrator to make an announcement for the students to "Please sit down!"

Sure. You betcha! It goes without saying that this announcement brought out a chorus of resounding "boos and hisses." The students never did sit down except, maybe, for a timeout.

There came a big moment for Don and the sold-out Mac Court in 1970. The UCLA Bruins came to town ranked very high in national polls, having finished the previous season as the NCAA national champions!

The hanging scoreboard over the pavilion looked like a bouncing yo-yo as it responded to a jam-packed rollicking, yelling, swaying, boisterous crowd of Duck basketball enthusiasts. Some thought that big box would come crashing down on the floor. It didn't. The building seemed to shake with all the bedlam going on inside.

So, what happened? The Ducks slew the Dragon Bruins, 78-65! Students flooded the court after the game, and as Don quaintly put it, "A highlight night for me as well as for Duck basketball." This victory was a benchmark for the final two years of the Stan Love era. The team didn't make it to the NCAAs but they did beat the rival OSU Beavers two out of three times, losing to them at Portland's Far West Basketball Classic.

Steve Belko, Oregon's coach for 14 years, retired and in came the era of "Kamikaze" basketball headed by Coach Dick Harter, who christened another moniker on the old building: "The Pit." Harter was the first to use this appellation for Mac Court, and the name stuck.

Harter's first year at the Duck helm did actually turn out to be the pits and not a very notable one for Don to announce: the home team went 6-20 and didn't win a single conference game.

The following year Ronnie Lee arrived from Boston and basketball frenzy again became the vogue in Eugene. It was during this roundball mania when Wichita State came to visit and their coach said of the Webfoots, "They come after you like a squad of Kamikazes."

A new uniqueness emerged as the Ducks became known as the "Kamikaze Kids." They carried that moniker for the next seven years of Harter's reign, and Don's game introductions came with this latest identity for the Ducks.

The reborn success of Duck basketball resulted in game sellouts which brought a resurgence to the old building. That enthusiasm resulted in the addition of end zone second and third-level balconies for the now-named "Pit." And, guess what? Stabilizers were added to the building in hopes that the old structure wouldn't shake and quake so much during the frenzy of a game going on inside.

All the excitement of the games brought a novel, but not too popular tradition; the throwing of frisbees by the students before the start of games. As many as 20-30 frisbees would spin through the electrified air in Mac Court, all at one time!

When the teams came up onto the floor Don would have to announce, "Okay, now it's time to stop the throwing!" Once, when Don was making his announcement, a free-flying Frisbee caught him square on the bridge of his nose. This made for a difficult night of announcing with a swelling, puffed-up proboscis.

An aftermath of the Frisbee fracas with the students was a paper frisbee, made from a popcorn box. It was placed on Don's announcing booklet and was transcribed with this message, "For the unreasonable regulation of a relatively harmless activity." You betcha! The anonymous donor obviously had never been cracked on the nose with a round, flying plastic missile.

Another sobriquet for the infamous basketball followers at UO came from UCLA coach Gene Bartow when he assessed that those people in "The Pit" were a "bunch of deranged idiots!" The Duck house jumped on that one, and the marketing geniuses came up with buttons and posters depicting the designation.

UO student, Ken Hoiland, was the one starting up this hullabaloo. He showed up at the games adorned with a cowboy hat and toy guns strapped to his sides. He had a black mask to cover his eyes and he rode a stick horse around the court to the student band's playing of the "William Tell Overture," theme song for the "Lone Ranger." Don played along with the act by introducing Ken's charade as the "Lone Deranger."

There were many games during the Harter era when students

camped out for days in front of the Pit to guarantee themselves tickets for the game.

Again in 1974 UCLA came to Eugene after winning the NCAA National Championships. They had just been upset by the Oregon State Beavers in Corvallis and were definitely looking to redeem themselves with a win over the Ducks. All this hoopla led Don to what he says was one of the biggest faux pas he ever made "in my entire announcing career!"

As Don was getting into his introductions of the teams, first UCLA, he was thinking, "NCAA" and "Defending Champions." Out came his UCLA presentation: "And now the starting lineup for the descending, er, uh; I mean, the defending national champions!"

The fans in the arena went bananas and as luck would have it, Oregon won the game 56-51. Covering the game that night for the *Portland Oregonian* newspaper was sports writer Leo Davis who made special note of Don's indiscretion in the next day's paper.

The Daisy Ducks, a women's booster organization for the university, changed the usual format for halftime activities. They started up Daisy Duck Bingo as a method of raising money to go toward athletic scholarships.

Don recaps the story of a mother and her young son who had won $650 in a Daisy Ducks' bingo game. She had her boy punch out the numbers on the card as they were called out. After they won the youngster was positively ecstatic with their shared good fortune. He went with his mom to collect the money at the scorer's table. Don was the numbers caller.

Now race forward to the next home game. Don had laryngitis and Roger Terrall, announcer for the women's games for many years, stood in for him. At this game the mother-son team that had won the previous bingo match failed miserably this time, not getting a single number on their card. Bad day at black rock! The young lad was totally disappointed, saying to his mother, "I don't like this Don Essig!" Oh, well. Such are the perceptions of young people when things don't exactly turn out the way they were perceived.

As mentioned earlier, was the fact that students stood during the games which was a major impediment to the press corps and for Don's announcing. In the 1990s, the lower sections in Mac were remodeled seating the students on just one side, then redoing the other three sides to make room for reserved seating for the donors.

This was a major change for Don. He was moved to the floor at court-side, sitting next to scorebook keeper, Mark Bloom. It was a good move for the public address announcer, but it did come with some drawbacks. Many times during games Don's view was blocked by a coach or an official moving directly into his line of vision.

The move did allow him to see more of the action on the floor, and he did enjoy the ongoing commentary proffered by coaches and referees during the game. However, it sometimes did interfere with his game observations. Too bad for you, Don. Game management sometimes giveth, and sometimes they taketh away!

Don occasionally brought his magic mike to some women's games. He was also recruited to voice men's gymnastics meets. At the time Oregon was recognized as a national power in men's gymnastics under Coach Bill Ballester. Don enjoyed learning to pronounce the names of the Japanese and Romanian team members when they came to Mac to perform. He placed a number of phonetic notes next to the names on his program to help him with the pronunciations. A prominent moment in this announcing assignment was working the three-day NCAA Championships held in Mac Court. He also public addressed two PAC-10 Conference championship meets. Gymnastics was dropped at Oregon in the 1970s because of budget cuts.

For over half of the 84 years of existence of McArthur Court, Don Essig's voice rumbled through the halls of this hallowed arena. During this time he had announced through the tenures of thirteen athletic directors, seven basketball coaches, five sports information directors and nine radio play-by-play announcers!

That's thirty-four different personages connected to the old building — but the same voice in old Mac Court.

Above: Don & Janet in Autzen PA booth

Right: Stan, Don and Jack, 2010

Above: Autzen Stadium

Right: Don at Rose Bowl pep rally, 2010

CHAPTER THIRTEEN

The Man in the Sky

"And the weather report for today's game,
"It never rains in Autzen Stadium!."

—Don Essig
PA Announcer

When PAC-12 Commissioner Larry Scott announced the conferences first championship game to be played in the year 2011 at Autzen Stadium on the University of Oregon campus, he also presented another first. Don Essig, for the first time in recent memory, would not be public address announcing a Duck home football game! Instead, Paul Olden, announcer for the New York Yankees baseball team would take over the stadium microphone. Olden's previous experience included 12 Super Bowl games.

Hometown fans were not pleased with the decision. Don was introduced and allowed to lead the fans in his now popular, "It never rains in Autzen Stadium." For the rest of the game he was left standing behind the guest announcer in the PA booth.

Asking Don today about his career as a public address announcer, his response: "It has been and is a great ride; a tremendous and unique hobby. It's just about the best hobby anyone could have."

Few people ever get this kind of opportunity to arena-announce any athletic event and Don has ridden it to the max.

He could have added that people do not necessarily get into this kind of activity for the money. Few would call it a full time job, except, of course, someone like Olden.

Webster's Dictionary defines the word hobby as "a pursuit of interest engaged in for relaxation." Sports game savants would have to take a double-take on that definition for a public address announcer! It is fairly obvious one would not always call it a relaxing activity. Still, Don never considered it a job. It was a professional involvement inasmuch as he did receive some remuneration; monetary, plus other extra benefits.

The fun of announcing far outweighed any stresses the job might entail, Don insists. Thus, one would suppose stepping into the press box booth, grabbing a microphone, and keeping the spectators in the arena up to snuff on the rudiments of the game, was a hobby and not just another job.

Over the years Don has been placed on the Oregon athletic department's staff list. He has been included as part of the many fund-raising activities around the state, which included golf and dinner dates. He and Janet have gone on various trips with the teams as guests of the athletic department, plus they have received tickets to Bowl games and trips to the PAC-12 basketball tournament. Don says he and Janet have received many benefits by being formally included with the department's staff. He feels the department has been good for his family for all the time and effort he put in, on behalf of the Duck athletic program. For all this he says he is most proud and satisfied to be part of the University's athletic family.

Don has had a variety of experiences in his some 45 years manning the mike at Duck athletic affairs. He and friend Jack Pynes, who was a spotter for him from the very first game, acquired another friend to help in the booth, Roger Diddock. When Roger moved on, Joe Wiseman filled in for him and did the job until he moved on and was replace by former football coach, Dick Arbuckle. Dick just lasted a year; he wanted a return to coaching.

Don had to find another spotter. Up popped Stan Hultgren, a longtime friend and colleague, as well as co-owner with Don and Janet of their vacation cabin up in the Cascade Mountains. He became the new man in the booth.

Since 1974, Stan, Jack and Don have become like a well-oiled machine in the announcing booth. This has become even more obvious with the honors and praise Don has received for the exemplary work that has taken place with the Autzen Stadium on-field broadcasting. Jack assists with what happens with the tackles as well as double-checking on who is participating in the game.

All this frees up Don to provide a running commentary of game information for the fans, providing briefs of the action on the field. Another responsibility is special stadium announcements and ad-lib requests, as a courtesy for those in attendance.

Don's accolades for his press box team was summed up: "Jack and Stan are the consummate professionals in the booth spotting a football game for the PA announcer."

As for Don, he picked up the exemplary description of PA "Voice of the Ducks," a title he has shared with another longtime radio play-by-play announcer, Jerry Allen. They refer to one another as the "Other Voice of the Ducks." They have often served as joint guest speakers or master of ceremonies at various and sundry athletic events.

After some 15 years into his announcing, Don's family presented him with a license plate holder with the engraving, "Voice of the Ducks." In keeping with, and furthering his "Don Duck" image, on his 50th birthday in 1988 his family again chipped in and presented him with a "Go Ducks" neon sign that hangs in the front window of their home.

The sign is loyally turned on for every men's football or basketball game. It's mysterious, and maybe ironic, that a continous string of winning football seasons, right up to the Ducks victory in the 2012 Rose Bowl game, all began with the lighting of that mystical green madstone! The victory was Oregon's first Rose Bowl win since 1917.

Obviously the family strongly believes that vivid green talisman is some sort of secret Webfoot weapon!

One of Don's earliest experiences as the PA man came in his second game in Autzen Stadium. The Ducks were playing the University of Idaho, which at the time was ranked very high in the country for passing yards per game. In the first half the Ducks essentially shut down the Vandals vaunted passing attack with very few yards allowed by halftime.

During the intermission break, one of the local television announcers, Hal Waymeyer, came into the booth and asked, "Don, do you have a live microphone?" Hal knew of what he spoke as he was also a part-time PA announcer for some Oregon State University events.

Don answered the query that he didn't think so because he had been turning it off and on for every play.

"Well," Hal countered, "I was down on the field during the first half and I could have sworn that I heard over the sound system the words, 'The Idaho passing attack isn't worth a crap today!'"

Without twisting on the button, Don blew into the mike. Sure enough out over the speakers came the "whooshing" sound, loud and clear, of Don blowing into the mike. At the time Don's microphone was on a stand pointing at him and in an off setting. The on-off switch obviously was not working.

From that day forward, Don said the mike came off the stand "to be forever held in my left hand, and pointed away from me, at all times, except when I am announcing". No more inadvertent announcements to the crowd just because the mike didn't shut down.

In the early years of announcing prior to the prevalence of cell phones and texting, there were a number of "special" announcements: notably, lost children and lost parents. Later it was discovered that some people liked to send up phony kid announcements just to hear their names spoken over the sound system.

Doctors to call their offices or answering services was another enigma. It was discovered that the same doctor was getting his name announced every game just so he could hear, as well as have many other people in the stands hear his name, maybe a great way to advertise his practice! So the athletic department started having the docs being registered before the game. They were given a "Doctor number" to be used if they were being paged.

Other announcements during those early years were related to automobiles located in the parking lot. One of many favorites concerned an abandoned car "with the lights on, the doors locked, and the motor running!" Don's press box crew concluded that the car owner probably had more than just a few "brewskies" at some tailgate party, and then left the drink-along quickly to get to the game.

It was these times Don loves to start the announcement, "Now, fans, today's lucky car license number is . . .".

One of the major changes that has taken place in football PA announcing is the influx of other non-game communications that were being made. In the beginning there might have been five or six five-by-eight cards with a few broadcast requests; maybe even other game scores, but few for special events publicity. Now the Athletic Department includes a marketing staff that provides an additional 15-page scripted announcement booklet to be read during game breaks and timeouts. A marketing staff member is included as part of Don's announcing crew in the booth to cue him when to give each non-game announcement.

The need to meet the ever-increasing athletic budget changed his role as the PA guy, significantly increasing the number of announcements during the game. The new big screen, "Duck Vision," now affixed in the stadium has most announcements being coordinated with the pictures or film showing on the screen. This just proves that all the changes in the athletic profession has to go with the acquisition of many more sponsors and more fund-raising activities to advertise.

Along with all the other changes the remolding and expansion of Autzen in 2003, included a new press box some 8 to 10 building stories above the field. This prompted the need for new binoculars to assist spotter Jack checking the uniform numbers.

There are other changes that have taken place affecting PA announcing. A new twist and a new problem for Don and his announcing crew involved the continuing change of uniform colors for the Ducks--even diverging into Oregon State's contrast color for orange, which is black. This dabbling into many contrasting football jersey and pants combinations made it difficult to call and report player and play situations.

For this game-viewing problem Don says he is especially thankful for his longtime spotter, Jack Pynes. "For most of the uniforms there is not a huge contrast in the colors. If I didn't have Jack with the field glasses we wouldn't be able to identify many of the players or their tackles at all!"

Jack has been a faithful back for Don since they first teamed up in 1968, missing only two games during that time! Stan Hultgren has only missed a few games during his tenure with Don as a spotter.

So, how about Don? He missed the 1984 game with Arizona State because of a herniated disc in his neck. The Ducks were blown out that day in a driving rainstorm! Don was at home listening to the game, as comfortably ensconced as his back pain would allow, on his living room sofa, where it never rains!

Would you believe he also once missed a quarter of a game?

A close family friend was getting married in Seattle at 7 p.m. the evening of an afternoon game in Autzen. Don told Sports Information Director Steve Helyear he couldn't do the game and needed a backup announcer.

Helyear decided he didn't want to announce so he went out and located a Duck booster who had an airplane. The arrangement he made was to have the volunteer pilot seated next to announcer Don for the first three quarters of the game. A local high school game announcer was sought out and commissioned to cover the last quarter. This freed up Don and his pilot to take off for Seattle.

The aftermath? Don was at the church, got out of his "Go Duck" clothes and was ready for the ceremony -- before any of the family had even arrived. He had one fast pilot!

Getting back to Pynes, standing tall for the man behind the mike; his professed faith is Catholic. Don is a devout Congregationalist Protestant.   Jack recalls with pride when Oregon played

Notre Dame in Autzen: "I enjoyed the Notre Dame game, having grown up a Catholic boy. Before the game Don kept teasing me about his having a thing about not allowing any Catholic spotters in the booth."

The kidding about their religious affiliations has been ongoing throughout all their announcing-spotting years together. After the Notre Dame game, Jack dragged out of his carryall bag a bottle of red wine and a small bag of fish crackers. Don implied that he was probably planning to celebrate a big Notre Dame victory. Unfortunately, for Don, the Ducks were not very good that season finishing with a season record of 2-8-1. They gave up a field goal to the fighting Irish in the last minute; the game ending in a 16-16 tie. To no one's surprise, the announcing crew stayed on and celebrated anyway, before an empty house.

The legacy for Don as a PA announcer had its beginning in the 1980s. At the time Athletic Director Bill Byrne sent out a directive that there would be no more smoking in the stadium stands during the games. OK, that sounded reasonable. Along with this edict was the order that they were not going to allow any more open umbrellas in the stands, either. To make sure everyone going to the games knew of this mandate, Don was given the responsibility to read this new exposition at each of the home football games.

Over time, in hopes of sprucing up the proclamation, which was often read during early fall games when there was no rain, Don began including at the end of each announcement, "Not to worry. Don't even think about umbrellas because it never rains in Autzen Stadium anyway."

This sounded ludicrous because during the 1960s, 1970s, and early 1980s, it seemed to rain for just about every home game. The same situation was occurring at the sister institution some 50 miles north at Oregon State University in Corvallis! The Beaver school, however, didn't put a ban on umbrellas in Parker Stadium.

Back in Eugene, Don eventually concluded his pre-game prognostication with, "As you know, the real weather report is . . . . It never rains in Autzen Stadium!" In actuality, from this point on the Ducks went nearly eleven years without a rainy game! In Oregon? It's unbelievable!

It wasn't long before the fans began yelling en-masse, the "Never rains in Autzen" mantra along with him. Today, regardless of whether it is raining or not, it has become a part of the weather report at the beginning of all home games, blaring throughout the stadium! It has become Don Essig's signature statement.

Following two rainy games in the late 2000s, Don wanted to give up the announcement. Associate Athletic Director Dave Heeke told him not to stop making it. Heeke said that by now the announcement really had nothing to do with the weather. It had become a part of the ambiance of Autzen Stadium. The real meaning was typical Don Essig: everyone in the crowd was having a good time and it was always a "sunny" experience to be a Duck fan!

Today in Eugene and throughout Oregon people can be heard expounding, "Hey, it never rains in Autzen Stadium!" Of course Don gets the credit, or the blame, for the aphorism. It all depends on positioning in the state: down-valley, mid-valley Webfootville, or Beaver Country.

In 2005 Don had T-shirts printed with the "never rains" logo printed on the front. He engaged, he didn't have to persuade, the Oregon Duck cheerleaders to sell them. All the profits from selling the shirts were to go to the cheerleader travel fund. Close to $7,000 was realized from the venture. The cheerleaders were most grateful.

Don describes an unexpected meeting he had with a woman when he was approached by her at one of the Big Green Benefit Auction dinners to get donors for a scholarship program. The lady wanted to tell him about her five-year-old grandson. The little boy had been attending Duck football games since he was two weeks old! (Wow! Talk about recruiting them early!)

It was a Saturday morning, the sky was pretty much dark and cloudy. The boy's mother told him they wouldn't be going to the game because the weather looked bad, and it probably would be wet and cold. The grandson responded, "But Mom, the man in the sky says it never rains in Autzen Stadium!"

To Don it was not only a great testimonial to him, but yet another label for the announcer, "The man in the sky!"

Hey, wait a minute Don. Isn't that being a little bit presumptuous? It did substantiate the perceptions of a five-year-old about the PA speakers in the stadium, and where all those announcements came from. But, after all!

What is needed here is a postscript to the story. At church the next morning Don told his minister, Pastor Greg Flint, that he found out at a dinner he had attended the night before that there were actually "two of us that people could now look up to." Uh huh, sure, you betcha!

A final post script for this section is that, although Don did not announce football games in Autzen Stadium the first year it opened in 1967, in the intervening years of his being behind the mike he has announced for and outlasted six different Duck football coaches!

A big disappointment for Don in his announcing career began in 1988. Having worked high school games and being a high school principal, he pretty much figured out he knew what was necessary to do a good job in announcing high school football and basketball games.

He put together all his ideas and composed a small book he titled, "The Unseen Voice: How To an Effective Public Address Announcer." His intent was to sell this project to a sponsor and have it sent free to all the high school athletic directors across the country. He perceived that the booklet could then be used to help fledging high school announcers, many of whom are students, to find out the techniques and rudiments to make them successful as game-side announcers.

Again, friend Dennis Arendt provided the artwork. The book went to press, but without any sponsors to underwrite the project. Don maintains a few copies of the book. He says he could probably wallpaper his bathroom with the rejection letters he received from various businesses and organizations he tried recruiting as sponsors.

He is still quite proud of the fact that he wrote the book. He says that his book is very colorful, and, on occasion some people still inquire if there are any books available to buy.

Don sent Brad Rumble at the National Association of Sports Public Address Announcers a rundown of all he accomplished in his hobby-to-end-all-hobbies over the past 50 years. The listing does not include the many football and basketball banquets he participated in with the UO men's teams, or any of a wide assortment of fundraising events that he became a part of with the UO athletic department.

Above: Don's plaque. Honorary membership in UO letterman's club, 2009

University of Oregon Announcing Events December, 1967 to March, 2012

Football: 286
Frosh/JV Football: 7
Spring FB Games: 14
Basketball: 686 (Men's 677, Women's 9)
Men's Gymnastics: 42
Baseball: 2
Total University of Oregon Events: 1,037

Other Team Announcing Occasions

Oregon City & Sheldon High School Games: 88
NCAA Basketball Tournament Games: 8
Portland's Far West Basketball Classic Games: 204
Professional Tennis Exhibition: 1
NIT Basketball Tournament Games: 4
Portland Trailblazers Basketball Games: 7
Eugene Emeralds Baseball Games: 6
Eugene Bombers Semi-pro Football Games: 10
Other Events Total: 328

Total Events Announced: 1,365 November, 1961 - March, 2012

CHAPTER FOURTEEN

Don Essig's Announcing Statistics

"At the end of the day, I'm very convinced that you're going to be judged on how you are as a husband and father, and not on how many bowl games (you) won."

—Urban Meyer
College Football Coach

D on says he will always proclaim the acme of his announcing career came at the October, 2009, University of Oregon Athletic Hall of Fame dinner when he was awarded an Honorary Lifetime Membership in The Order of the O, the UO's athletic department lettermen's club.

Another honor he will cherish was his 1995 Oregon Club Len Casanova Lifetime Achievement Award for his many years of devoted time to the Oregon Club of Eugene-Springfield.

In 2010, Don was given a membership in the National Association of Sports Public Address Announcers. And in 2012, he became an official member of NASPAA's one-thousand event group.

Not too bad of a hobby—this public address announcing gig!

Above: Don's family from left to right, Holly, Ted, Brother Marcus, Nancy Essig, Scott, (Ducky) Kim, Sister Natalie, George Cantrell, Janet and Don

Above: Don's immediate family from left to right, Brother Marc, Sister Natalie, Mother Natalie, Father Milton and Don

Post Script by the Author

My wife, Joanne, and I have known Don and Janet Aune Essig since our undergraduate days at Oregon State College. Janet was definitely my idea of a poster calendar girl, as well as one fine looking Wrestling Queen. In my narcissistic mind Don was lucky to get Janet. What saved him from my courting her was the fact that I was already married and Joanne would not have taken kindly to my going out with some college coed!

Don and Janet's two sons, Scott and Ted, are the same age as our two children, son Eric and daughter Kristen. We raised our families within close proximity to each other. We still feel so familiar with the Essigs that to this day, Don and Janet are still referred to as "Unca Don" and "Aunt Janny" in our family.

Their oldest, and our Godson, Scott, is a "go-getter", an entrepreneur, much into the mode of his father. He and his wife, Kim, own and operate a promotions company, Essig Entertainment. One of their primary obligations is to fill the Moshofsky Center at Autzen Stadium with hundreds of tables and chairs for the athletic fans who come to the center before games, and during halftime at football games. Don and Janet assist Scott and Kim's crew setting up as well as breaking down all this equipment. It is later stored in warehouse facilities in Eugene awaiting use at other big gatherings in Eugene and surrounding areas.

Ted is the laid-back son, which is also true of his wife Holly. They present a more of a "give-or-take" attitude. Both their smiles and outward warmness exemplifies their "Hi, there; it's great seeing you again" way of looking at things. Ted is an accomplished guitar player who has performed with country-western bands in Oregon. He likes to brag about the time he once played guitar with country music star, Jimmy Buffett. Ted also operates his own painting business in Eugene. Holly is employed by a large medical practice in Eugene.

It's kind of ironic that Don was into his teaching career in public schools while I was working in the Oregon State University Athletic Department. Later, after doing some graduate work at the UO, I went into public school teaching. Don, by now, had reversed the field, not only as a full-time educator, but also began doing work for the University of Oregon athletic department!

Ah, well, such is life. Times and circumstances change; sometimes a lot. Even though we progress, we still stick to our core values and beliefs. Nothing remains the same, nor should it. Like they say, the only things we can really be sure of in this life are paying taxes, dying, and, as long as Don Essig is the Duck public address announcer, "It'll never rain in Autzen Stadium!"

Chuck Wenstrom

About the Author

Following United States Air Force service during the Korean conflict Chuck Wenstrom attended Oregon State College graduating in 1960 with a bachelor's, and later a master's degree in 1971 in education. He worked for the Oregon State System of Higher Education as a director of information in Portland. He returned to Oregon State University as Assistant Alumni Director and Editor of *The Oregon Stater* alumni magazine. He also was assistant sports information director for the athletic department. A follower of sports and being a former sports official prompted him to write his first book, *Referee: Staying Up to Snuff. It Never Rains in Autzen Stadium* is his second endeavor and is in the general area of sports announcing.